FASHION FILES
Fashion Marketing and PR

FASHION FILES
Fashion Marketing and PR ^{FF}

MARIA COSTANTINO

BT Batsford Ltd London

Printed in China

for the publishers

BT Batsford Ltd

583 Fulham Road

London SW6 5BY

www.batsford.com

ISBN 0 7134 8334 2

A CIP catalogue record for this book is
available from the British Library.

CONTENTS

INTRODUCTION   6

THE CONSUMER   22

THE RAW MATERIALS   34

MARKETING METHODS   46

BRANDS AND BRANDING   60

PLANNING AHEAD   72

PUBLIC RELATIONS   82

READING LIST   94

PICTURE ACKNOWLEDGEMENTS   95

INDEX   96

INTRODUCTION

The fashion industry – from the production of raw materials to the distribution of the finished goods – accounts for an estimated one third of the world's economy. In the USA alone, one in every eight workers is employed in fashion, while in the UK the fashion/textile industry is the nation's fourth largest.

As in all other industries, the goal of the fashion industry is to make a profit, and like all other industries there are winners and losers: with losses of £23 million (c. $37 million), 400 F. W. Woolworth five-and-dime stores are to close across the USA, ending a century-old business. The only remaining Woolworth-owned stores are in Mexico and Germany, since the 781 British Woolworth's stores are owned by Kingfisher. Meanwhile, Britain's trendiest shirtmaker, Ted Baker – a company now worth an estimated £56 million (c. $89 million) – is to be floated on the stockmarket in its efforts to become a global brand.

Like all other contemporary businesses, the fashion industry has become market-oriented: it no longer dictates what its customers should wear, and importantly, it is no longer elitist, even though the elite design and manufacturing system of *haute couture* continues.

THE ORIGINS OF FASHION

Until the late Middle Ages in Europe, fashion as we understand it today did not exist and dress was a form of regional costume. With the emergence of royal and princely courts, the rise of cities and city states and the accompanying expansion in international trade, the fourteenth century saw the beginnings of distinctions between traditional dress and an increased aristocratic interest in fashionable clothing. As political and economic power shifted from one geographic region to another, so fashion developed in a number of centres, and as one of the valuable trade commodities of the period was the primary substance of fashion, cloth itself became a symbol of wealth. For the first time the practice of discarding outdated rather than outworn clothes became current.

THE FRENCH COURT

France's emergence as a fashion capital was based largely on the primary market of textiles established during the reign of Louis XIV. To

Madame de Pompadour (1721–1764), mistress of King Louis XV of France, depicted here by François Boucher. As a fashion leader she gave her name to a hairstyle and to the pattern of brightly-hued small flowers or bouquets used in textile design.

The 'Queen of Fashion', Marie Antoinette (1755–1793). As wife of Louis XVI of France, she was the most influential fashion leader of the eighteenth century and was dressed by the first named *couturier*, Rose Bertin.

meet the growing interest in and demand for the fine fabrics that were worn at the royal court of Versailles, Louis established textile production in Lyons and lace manufacturing at Alençon. During the eighteenth century, while the French kings Louis XV and Louis XVI continued to encourage and support the French industries, a shift in the focus of fashion occurred.

While the wealthy and aristocratic man remained extravagantly dressed, continuing to sport silk hose, wigs, hats and even cosmetics, the fashion leaders were women, notably those such as Madame de Pompadour, Madame du Barry and Queen Marie Antoinette, the wives and mistresses of the French kings. Marie Antoinette's wardrobe was reported to have filled three large rooms at Versailles, and it has been suggested that she might have escaped the guillotine had she not insisted on attempting to flee France encumbered by several large wardrobe trunks of her clothes which slowed her passage through the countryside!

The reign of Marie Antoinette as the 'queen of fashion' was to affect the development of the modern fashion industry, for it is in this period that we see the emergence of a named *couturier*, Rose Bertin, and with this emergence, a different relationship between client and *couturier*. Where customers had previously dictated to the *couturier* their stringent demands regarding fashionable clothing, Bertin – largely because the queen was a shy, 16-year-old Austrian girl – turned the tables and began to impose her own ideas on her clients. Bertin, who was later awarded the official title of Minister of Fashion,

persuaded the young queen to adopt an informal style of dress associated with shepherdesses as well as the elaborate hair styles that so typified the last years of the eighteenth century.

The first models

With the splendour of the French court setting the benchmark for women's fashions throughout Europe, Bertin may be counted as the first *couturier* of international repute, and one device she employed to maintain her dominance in matters of style throughout Europe was the fashion doll. Dolls dressed in exquisite miniature versions of complete outfits could easily be sent be abroad for client approval.

The use of such miniature models as marketing tools has largely disappeared, and in their place today we have the living dolls of the fashion industry: the models and supermodels who travel the world, either in person to grace the international catwalks or as media images in magazines and on television. Bertin's fashion dolls also endure in the form of Barbie and Sindy dolls whose looks and wardrobe closely follow contemporary fashion trends and inform the world's pre-teenage girls of notions of feminine beauty. Not surprisingly, it is now possible to have a Sindy doll modelled on the face and figure of supermodel Naomi Campbell, with exclusively designed doll's wardrobes by the likes of Vivienne Westwood and Jean-Paul Gaultier. And when girls have outgrown Barbie and Sindy, their place is taken by shop mannequins: Adel Rootstein designs and produces mannequins based on the features of the well-known models of the day.

The modern equivalent of Rose Bertin's fashion dolls. Mannequins produced by Adel Rootstein are life-size replicas of contemporary fashion models.

POST-REVOLUTIONARY INFLUENCES

After the French Revolution, the emerging French fashion industry was halted in its tracks: Bertin herself was forced to flee France, and although she returned in 1800 to re-establish her business, she was never to regain her former status. Not surprisingly, revolutionary politics had ushered in a phase of 'plain dressing' – a trend that, in menswear at least, had been growing since the mid-eighteenth century.

In England, those men who continued the use of elaborate lace, feathers and brightly coloured silks as opposed to more sombre wools ran the risk of being attacked as a 'French Dog', as elaborate menswear became associated with the corruption of the French court. Such sentiments were also shared in America:

although 'Yankee Doodle Dandy', the song about the man who 'stuck a feather in his cap and called it Macaroni', was originally written by an Englishman to make fun of the poorly dressed American Revolutionary soldiers, it was adopted by the American colonies in a growing distaste for the foppish and effete French fashions.

In France itself during the post-Revolutionary period of the Directoire [c1790-1804], many Frenchmen and women also began to distance themselves from the courtly ways of dress. Women favoured the styles influenced by

Empress Josephine (1763–1814), wife of Napoleon I, was dressed by L.H. Leroy in the appropriately-named 'Empire' look, popular in Europe and America around 1795–1820.

Classical Greece and Rome that were 're-invented' and promoted by L.H. Leroy, who dressed the Empress Josephine, while the new masculine ideal was based on the concept of the 'English Country Gentleman' – a man not necessarily of noble birth, but one who had perhaps acquired learning, gentle manners and had elevated himself above the 'mob' in politics, thought and actions.

THE RISE OF ENGLISH FASHION

In England, even the Prince of Wales, later the Regent and the future George IV, preferred more sober below-the-knee breeches, boots and the dark tail coat that was to become formal dress for many men right through the early years of the twentieth century. These garments had been refined and promoted by Beau Brummell, and it was a fashion that did much to encourage the rise of English tailoring to the international status that it continues to enjoy today. Savile Row tailor Henry Poole was known to accept invitations to elite social events in lieu of payment (many gentlemen went into debt on account of their wardrobe!), and at one such event he met the exiled French prince Louis Napoleon, who was raising funds to pay for his campaign to regain power. Poole – a mere tailor – was reputed to have lent the prince some £30,000 ($50,000)! Consequently, Poole was named official Court Tailor during the Second Empire.

While France was to re-emerge as a centre for women's fashions, London's Savile Row would retain the distinction of being the fashion centre

for menswear – at least until the mid-twentieth century when the rise of ready-to-wear, the emergence of new young Italian and American menswear designers and the 'Peacock Revolution' of the 1960s were to wake up and shake up the menswear industry.

Poole was not the only Englishman to rise to fame in France during the Second Empire: Charles Frederick Worth, another British tailor, was to become the official fashion designer to the Empress Eugénie. Often called the 'Father of French Fashion', Worth is credited with the first use of live *couture* mannequins (models) to display his creations and with being the first *couturier* to select and supply fabrics for a particular design (previously, clients had provided their own fabrics for *couturiers* to make up) and to prepare hand-coloured portfolios of designs for each of his clients.

LA CHAMBRE SYNDICALE DE LA COUTURE

It was Worth's son, Gaston, who in 1868 was to initiate the *Chambre Syndicale de la Couture*, an organization to co-ordinate the activities of the growing couture industry and to limit competition. This organization was to develop into the *Fédération Française de la Couture*, which includes the three branches of the *Chambre Syndicale de la Couture Parisienne* which promotes and protects *couture*; the *Chambre Syndicale de Prêt-à-Porter*, an association of the ready-to-wear branches of the *couture* houses and the 'best of the rest' of French ready-to-wear, and the *Chambre*

London's Savile Row c.1890. Henry Poole and Co., the oldest established firm of tailors on the street, was founded in 1806.

Syndicale de la Mode Masculine, an association of the menswear industries of *couture*. Membership of the *Couture-Creation* list, in which designers are officially recognized as *couturiers*, is decided on by a special government commission of the Department of Industry, and applicants to join the list must fulfil a number of requirements.

Couturiers must have their workrooms in Paris and employ at least 20 people who carry out their work wherever possible by hand and in the highest traditions of craftsmanship. Furthermore, all work except for specialist tasks like beading or embroidery must be undertaken 'in-house'. All *couture* garments must be custom-made and individually fitted to each

Couture on show at the House of Yves Saint Laurent. Increasingly unprofitable, *couture* nevertheless adds prestige to diffusion lines and licensed goods like cosmetics and perfumes.

client; sketches for garments must be made only by the house designer, and garments from the collection must remain exactly as they were designed – designs may not be altered to suit a particular client.

Twice a year, in January and July, each *couture* house must show a collection of at least 75 models (outfits) on live mannequins, three of whom must be employed throughout the year.

In return, the *Chambre Syndicale de la Couture Parisienne* is responsible for the scheduling and co-ordination of dates and times of *couture* showings for buyers and the press. It issues invitations and press cards, arranges shipping dates to ensure that all models are sent to retailers and to manufacturers who are permitted to produce 'couture copies' on the same date (approximately thirty days after the show date) and it sets the official release date for press photos and sketches to coincide with the arrival of the ready-to-wear copies in stores (about six weeks after the show). The *Chambre* also regulates copying conditions: currently manufacturers and retailers who buy original models may sell copies in their own countries but they are not allowed to sell paper patterns. In their efforts to protect *couture* designs and prevent piracy – at least in France – the *Chambre* registers all new designs by listed French *couture* houses.

THE RISE OF READY-TO-WEAR

Despite the *Chambre Syndicale*'s efforts to maintain the authority of *couture* in dictating fashion, by the mid-twentieth century it was apparent that *couture* was no longer the leading force in matters of style. The rise of American and European ready-to-wear meant that by the end of 1977 all the members of the exclusive French *Couture-Creation* list (with the exception of Madame Alix Grès, who was President of the *Chambre Syndicale* at the time) had produced a *prêt-à-porter* collection. By 1979, Madame Grès herself added a ready-to-wear arm to her business as *couture* became increasingly unprofitable.

Today, the cost of presenting a *couture* collection can be as high as £2.5 million ($4 million), and subsequent sales from the estimated thousand *couture* customers world-wide do not return the initial outlay. Consequently, the losses from *couture* are balanced against profits from franchised boutiques, *prêt-à-porter* sales, designer-name fragrances and cosmetics and from licensed products like hosiery, sunglasses, underwear or even – as in the case of Pierre Cardin's portfolio of licensed goods bearing his name – canned fruit, baby strollers and the restaurant chain Maxim's, which now has a branch in Moscow.

Nevertheless, the continued existence of *haute couture* does serve some purpose: in addition to *couture*'s role as a 'laboratory of ideas', it also adds prestige to a range of loss-leader products like perfumes, cosmetics and accessories as well as to the less expensive off-

Pierre Cardin licenses his name to a range of non-fashion-related goods including canned fruit and wet suits and is associated with over 500 factories worldwide.

the-peg, mass-produced ready-to-wear lines designed and sold under the house name. While a Chanel or Dior *couture* dress may cost anything up to £30,000 ($50,000), a bottle of Chanel No.5 or Miss Dior *eau de toilette* carries the cachet of *couture* elegance without such a hefty price tag.

THE IMPACT OF INDUSTRIALIZATION

The fact that the aspiration to be fashionable is not restricted to society's elite is nothing new and not something that is easily overlooked by today's industry. The 'democratization of fashion' that has occurred in many ways parallels the decline in authority of *couture*, and began when the mass production of clothing became possible with the introduction of new technologies like the sewing machine.

A French tailor called Thimmonier patented a chain-stitch machine in 1829 that so upset the other French tailors that they rioted and smashed all the machines. The American Walter Hunt refined the design of the sewing machine in 1832 but made the terrible mistake of not patenting his design, therefore allowing credit for the invention of a hand-powered sewing machine to pass to Elias Howe in 1846. Isaac Singer, later to become a household name, developed the foot treadle and mass-produced his machines so that by 1867 he was producing 1,000 Singer sewing machines a day.

A logical development of the sewing machine was the introduction of paper patterns. These were first displayed in 1850 in Philadelphia by Ellen and William Demorest, and following their initial success they launched the quarterly magazine *Madame Demorest's Mirror of Fashion* in 1860, from which patterns of the French-inspired fashions of the day depicted in the magazine could be ordered by mail.

The home-sewing industry paved the way for future developments in the ready-to-wear industry when in 1863 Ebenezer Butterick, the founder of the Butterick Pattern Company, developed the concept of grading patterns (duplicating a style in a variety of sizes) which was adopted by manufacturers to develop and evolve their own patterns. As fit was perfected, so the stigma of ready-to-wear clothing (as

opposed to being able to afford hand-made clothing) began to diminish, particularly as more and more prestigious shops and department stores realised the huge potential market and began to stock and advertise ready-to-wear clothes. It is no wonder that at this time the French *couturiers* closed ranks to defend themselves against the onslaught of cheap, mass-produced copies!

THE ROLE OF TECHNOLOGY

Technological developments have played their part in advancing modern mass-production methods to the extent that mass-produced copies of *couture* styles can now be available within a few weeks of a fashion show – 24 hours after Sarah, Duchess of York left Westminster Abbey on her wedding day in 1986, a copy of her wedding dress was on display in an Oxford Street store window. Developments in the mass media from early fashion photography to today's glossy magazines and Hollywood movies to video and MTV have all played their role in shaping the modern fashion industry.

These developments, alongside the social, political and economic changes that have occurred in the last two centuries or so – the changing roles of both men and women, the emergence of a youth culture and youth market, the increasing interest in sporting and leisure time pursuits, the emergence of strong sub-cultural groups as well as developments in retailing from mail-order to television home shopping and out-of-town malls – have contributed to a situation where to speak of a

The fashion industry today is not just about clothes. The giant chemical industries create the fragrances and cosmetics that complete 'the look', with names and faces such as those of Somali-born model Iman used to market the products.

single 'fashion industry' is misleading, since a number of related industries contribute to its shape and success. There are the giant chemical industries that create the designer fragrances and the fibre and textile producers who provide the 'raw materials' of fashion, and there are the garment manufacturers, wholesalers and retailers, the models and the press and all of the associated ancillary operations that today constitute the fashion industry, from forecasters and stylists to merchandisers and public relations companies.

THE MODERN MARKET

With the decline in income generated by *couture* alone, the model of business practice it offered was also seen as outmoded. The *couture* end of the fashion industries remains product- and sales-oriented: its function is to produce the finest quality merchandise, to persuade potential customers that a particular product is the 'best' and to encourage them to buy. Not only do *couturiers* dictate what their customers will wear, but *couture* customers must conform to the house's way of doing business, since the *Chambre Syndicale* regulates when customers can have new *couture* collection garments.

The post-Second World War period ushered in a buyer's market, and many industries, including the fashion industry, had radically to rethink their business philosophy. When *couturiers* responded to new market forces with *prêt-à-porter* lines, they were recognizing the fact that they now had to determine what customers wanted and then produce it. Furthermore, they now had to realize that these customers were much different to the handful of elite *couture* customers and had to acknowledge a shift in the designer–client relationship.

For these reasons, much of the fashion industry today is marketing-oriented: it gathers information from the marketplace and modifies its business methods to match the needs and wants of a large number of customers across the world. Despite the increasing gap between designer and consumer brought about by mass-

The Body Shop demonstrates part of the fashion industry's response to changes in the market place. Growing environmental concerns among consumers encouraged the Body Shop to adopt its non-exploitative approach: environmentally-friendly, natural ingredients, simple and affordable packaging and no testing on animals are part of its ethos.

production techniques, the focus of marketing is largely on the consumer's requirements, since the consumer is the ultimate destination of the industry's products.

THE ROLE OF MARKETING

Marketing involves exchange – usually of money, but can also be of time and effort on the part of the consumer in return for goods. We may spend more time and money in acquiring particular fashion items like designer-name watches, jewellery or sunglasses because we believe that such items have a greater value derived from their status as fashion items. This 'want-satisfying' power of a product is created by the marketers and is what economists call 'utility'.

At the heart of the marketing concept is the drive to satisfy consumers' needs, wants and demands: while we may *need* clothing to cover our bodies, to keep us warm and to protect us from the elements, what we *want* from clothing is for it to signify things about ourselves – our status, occupation, gender, age, class, lifestyle or whatever. And we *demand* to purchase those wants that we can afford.

Marketing has led to the development of new products and is responsible for bringing those products to consumers at a price they can afford. It is also responsible for the consumer being able to find the products in stores or to order them over the telephone or by mail, since part of marketing is the distribution of goods. Marketing also gives us information about products through advertising and publicity. Marketing, therefore, is known for 'The Four Ps':

product, price, promotion and place.

While many people still think of marketing as preying on the public's insecurities about their appearance and forcing them to buy goods they neither need nor can afford, one look at the rails full of discounted clothes left over at the end of the sales demonstrates all too well that marketers cannot *make* people buy! Nevertheless, marketing is the focus of the majority of fashion business's activity today, and it is the consumer who ultimately pays for it. It is claimed that for every pound, dollar, franc or yen that is spent in the marketplace, 50 per cent goes to cover the cost of bringing that product to the customer. But it is important to realize that marketing – particularly fashion marketing – also contributes to much of our contemporary culture: Reebok, Fila and Nike are among the companies who sponsor sports teams; Levi's gave us 'mini-films' in their television adverts like *Laundrette*; Benetton's ads encouraged public debate about art, advertising, politics, even life and death.

Where once the fine arts had the power to shock and outrage, fashion – both on its own and as part of a much wider popular culture – has largely assumed that role. After all, who can deny that the most popular cultural activity in the West is shopping!

To maintain market share, brand leaders like Louis Vuitton must spend millions of dollars worldwide promoting their name. The luxury leather goods company, part of the conglomerate that owns Boussac, Christian Dior and Givenchy, matches its sponsorship activities with suitably-high-class events such as yachting.

THE CONSUMER

Fashion begins and ends with the consumer, and no matter which part of the fashion industry a marketing-oriented organization works in, its primary task is to satisfy the consumer's or customer's needs and wants. But human needs extend beyond the basic physiological drives. Fashion transcends the basic human needs for protection and warmth: it gives us a means to express our personalities and identities as individuals, as part of larger social groups and in society as a whole. Thus our needs also give us the motivation to buy. Therefore, those fashion designers and fashion marketers who can understand our motivational drives often find that they can target their products more effectively and efficiently.

Consumer behaviour provides a number of concepts that help fashion marketers think about and understand their customers, and market research provides the techniques for measuring those concepts. Understanding consumers and their buying behaviour draws heavily on psychology, sociology and anthropology as well as cultural history. While all consumers are unique, each consumer shares some needs and wants with other consumers.

Apart from made-to-measure tailoring and *couture* outfits, most fashion marketing, including that of top-of-the-range designer ready-to-wear, involves providing standardized garments aimed at particular groups of consumers. Therefore, in order to market clothing in volume, groups of consumers with similar needs and wants have to be identified and supplied with similar products.

AGE

One of the main determinants of our buying behaviour is our age: lower birth rates in the 1960s and 1970s led to this period being called 'the zero population growth period'. In the 1980s, however, there was something of a 'baby boomlet' in both the USA and the UK, when a large number of women in their twenties and thirties decided to have children. In the 1990s, population in the West is growing slowly, and most demographers agree that this will continue

Fashion marketers now recognize the emergence of an important new trend: the 'greying' population. By 2050 it is estimated that 25 per cent of the population will be aged over 65. A few designers, like Issey Miyake, have acknowledged this potential market.

until around 2030. As a result, the fashion industry no longer expects population growth to be a significant determining factor in the future.

The average age of the population is also affected by increased life expectancy. In 1976, the median age in the USA was estimated at 28 years and 9 months. By the millennium, the median age of the US population is predicted to rise to 36 years and 9 months, and by the year 2030 it will reach 40 years and 8 months. This 'greying' of the population is not faced by the USA alone – it is a phenomenon experienced by countries throughout the Western world since the 1970s to the extent that it is believed that by the year 2050, people in the over-65 age group will outnumber those in the under-18 group. While the over-65s today account for around 12 per cent of the population, by 2050 this group will make up nearly 25 per cent. Fashion marketers now have their eyes set on the future as two important market trends begin to appear: the emergence of a much larger 'senior citizen' market, and a significant decline in the youth market. Consequently, designers and manufacturers will need to address not only the look of fashion clothing, but to rethink the sizing of garments to suit the older figure.

GENDER BALANCE

In addition to population changes and age, demographers also examine gender balance in society – the proportion of men to women at any one time, location, occupation, economic circumstances and social class. We may take it for granted, but gender is a very important factor affecting our choices in clothing and accessories. A careful look at advertising images, the media and even retail store layout will demonstrate that fashions are either feminine or masculine, and that there are very few genuinely 'unisex' fashion items.

LOCATION

Equally decisive on what we buy and how we buy is where we live, and in order for the fashion industry to market its products it must know how the population is distributed throughout the country. In the nineteenth century, the UK experienced a shift in the population from the countryside to the towns and cities as these became the centres of production and employment. More recently, rural areas and cities have seen their populations shift to suburban areas known variously as the 'commuter belts', 'urban sprawls' and 'edge cities'.

As people move from location to location, from north to south, or in the USA from state to state, lifestyles change, accompanied by changes in clothing needs, tastes and buying patterns. In order to service the needs of shifting populations, the fashion industry has to study these shifts and plan its marketing strategies accordingly. In the USA, which has seen a shift in the population from the colder northern states to the warmer southern states of the 'Sunbelt region', manufacturers have responded to the change by increasing their production and sale of warm-weather clothing. Meanwhile, retailers have responded to the shift to the suburbs with new store branches, and out-of-town

Shopping in a Singapore mall. Fashion marketers need information about age, gender, occupation and income but in the global market place each country's religious and cultural beliefs, as well as their economic status, must also be considered.

supermarkets have increased their size and range of clothing to suit these new needs.

WORK

Occupation also plays a role in determining what we buy and what we wear, since clothing reflects our professional status and also indicates that we belong to a particular occupational group. This century two major changes in occupation patterns have emerged. First, there has been a reduction in the number of blue-collar jobs (those that require manual or physical labour), while the number of white-collar jobs (those requiring technical skills or specialist services) has increased.

With women now constituting nearly half of the workforce, a major niche market is geared towards the 'career woman'. Liz Claiborne responded by designing complete wardrobes of mix and match separates.

The second change is in the number of women who work. In the USA, women now constitute 49 per cent of the entire workforce, and a major fashion market niche is now geared towards the career woman. The knowledge that the average working woman spends about 40 per cent more on clothing than non-working women is of primary interest to the fashion industry for a number of reasons. First, there is the type of clothing she will need: something 'sophisticated', 'professional' and good quality, in short, outfits that are 'smart'. Second, for these women who must divide their time between the demands of their careers and the demands of their home life, time itself is of great importance. Consequently, fashion marketers have responded with mail-order shopping via catalogues, magalogues and 'electronic' shopping.

Meanwhile, men's roles have also changed as a shortened working week has increased their participation in home life and in leisure activities. Consequently, men's wardrobes which were once restricted to the working suit, the 'Sunday Best' outfit and perhaps something more casual for weekend wear has expanded alongside their new activities. Consequently, as men now 'need' more clothes, they have become more fashion-conscious and, consequently, a growth market for the fashion industry.

WEALTH

Traditionally, society has been divided by income classes. In the past, it was the wealthiest in societies who were the most fashionable simply because they could afford to spend money on lavish clothes. Fashionable clothing thus became something of a status symbol rather than the expression of good taste, and consequently many consumers demonstrated their financial success by buying and wearing expensive clothing. Today's mass production of fashion means that fashion is more democratic: everyone can now enjoy fashionable clothing.

Yet buying power continues to be one of the most important influences on fashion, since goods are targeted at groups of people who have a certain amount of money to spend on them, and market researchers carry out demographic studies – statistical studies of the characteristics of populations – on behalf of textile producers, manufacturers and retailers to find out which segments of the population have the most buying power. Demographic characteristics will affect the type of clothing that we as individuals buy as well as exerting influence over the rational choices we make.

While gender, age and occupation all have their effect on just how much disposable income is available to be spent on fashion items, the consumer's spending power is largely determined by three factors: personal income, accumulated or net worth and available consumer credit. While our purchasing power (our personal income minus tax) has increased, the percentage of that purchasing power used to buy fashion

Consumers' values, attitudes and lifestyles can be translated into the visible and tangible. The interior of Gianni Versace's store reflects the notion that both the clothes and the customers are part of the same class and value system.

garments has decreased.

Many fashion companies continue to hold the belief that their competitors are companies who produce or sell the same types of goods as they do. There are other companies, however, who recognise that in order to capture a share of the market they must redefine their competition and compete with industries outside of their own for a share of the consumer's *discretionary income* – the income left after food, lodging and other necessities have been paid for. Discretionary income is not as straightforward as a salary: a consumer might be a high salary earner, but will still be less willing to spend their disposable income on fashion goods if they have small children to bring up.

CONSUMER PROFILES
Class

Closely linked to occupation and income but with wider implications in terms of purchase behaviour, particularly of fashion goods, is social class. Class continues to be important to the structure of society in spite of the narrowing of social differences over the years by education and employment. For fashion marketers, social class is still seen as one of the most reliable indicators of consumers' values, attitudes and lifestyles.

The most widely used system in the fashion market for determining social stratification or social class is based on the National Readership Survey, which uses the classification system of A, B, C1, C2, D and E:

A   the upper/upper-middle class, employed in the higher managerial and administrative professions

B   the middle class, employed in middle management, administration and the professions

C1   the lower-middle class, employed as supervisors, clerical and junior managers

C2   the skilled working class, employed as skilled manual labourers

D   the working class, semi-skilled and un-skilled manual workers

E   pensioners, casual workers, the unemployed and those in receipt of state benefits

While these commonly accepted descriptions of each class in the UK are helpful to marketers in so much as they assist them to place advertisements in different publications, in relation to fashion marketing these descriptions can be unreliable and misleading, as social class continues to be decided by the occupation of the head of the household or chief wage-earner, who is usually assumed to be male. A female lawyer (who would be categorized as Class B) who is married to a schoolteacher (categorized as Class C1) will be categorized as Class C1. Consequently, using this method of social stratification inevitably means that women's social class is often hidden.

Geodemographics

A newer system of classifying consumers draws on geographical location. ACORN is a system based on the census and categorization of neighbourhoods (ACORN is an acronym of A Classification Of Residential Neighbourhoods), and information is derived from statistical analysis of census variables to discover residential areas. The census data is often linked to survey data on purchasing behaviour and information on media usage: knowing the post code or zip code of a respondent, a market researcher can determine the geodemographic category.

ACORN has six categories and 17 groups which includes Affluent Executives in Family Areas down to Older People in Less Affluent Areas. Such geodemographic data is largely used by marketers for target marketing, media planning and setting sales targets by areas, forecasting and selecting new locations for new retail outlets although the heaviest users for the information are the mail order companies.

PSYCHOGRAPHY AND MOTIVATION

In addition to demographic data, fashion marketers also make substantial use of psychographic data – information on people's attitudes, values and beliefs as they affect behaviour. Although less exact than demography, psychography can help marketers understand what motivates consumers to buy products, how much their lifestyle affects their attitudes towards a particular product and contributes to their purchasing decisions.

Motivation can best be described as the 'inner force' that drives consumers towards their goals. One of the most often cited explanations of human motivation was developed in the 1930s by the psychologist Abraham Maslow, whose theory states that people have a hierarchical 'pyramid of needs'.

The most basic level is what Maslow termed the *physiological needs*. These are the 'bodily' needs: the instinctive 'animal reactions' to hunger or cold, for example. Physiological needs would prompt us to buy warm woollen clothing for winter, but someone who could not satisfy that need – someone with little money to spend – could not afford to have fashion considerations and would wear any clothing they could find. In the clothing market, it is often the second-hand and charity shops which allow customers to fulfil this basic need. At the same time, the same basic physiological need – for warm clothing – can also motivate a product search in a wealthy customer. However, with this customer, other needs in Maslow's hierarchy would also have to be satisfied.

The next level up the hierarchy of needs is what Maslow called *safety*, or the need in us to feel secure. These needs relate to both the physical and emotional: we all have the need to feel relatively safe or to be free from worry. Some of our apparel purchases will be motivated by our need for such safety or security, especially in the areas of children's clothing, nightwear, workwear and sportswear.

The third level in the hierarchy of needs is *social needs*, which encompass the needs we have for acceptance and a sense of belonging in our society or group. It is really the need we have for love – not just romantic love, but what the Greeks called *agape*, an all-pervasive love. These needs can exert an extremely powerful influence on our fashion purchases. As teenagers, it is important for us to have the 'right' clothes to be part of 'the gang'. But although it is often believed that this is just a passing teenage phase, in fact this need remains with us and is just as strong throughout our lives.

Maslow's next level is the need for *esteem and status* –the need for recognition from others, the desire to have a recognized place in society and the need to be regarded with respect. The need for esteem and status is one of the strongest motivating forces in fashion purchasing. A flick through any fashion magazine's advertising will reveal just how often fashion garments and accessories like designer watches appeal to this need in us.

At the top of Maslow's pyramid of needs is the need for *self-actualization* – better understood as 'the need to be your own person'. Often called the 'I did it my way' syndrome, the need to recognize and accept ourselves as we are, to have our own standards and to live up to them can be seen in the 'creative' dresser who has fulfilled all the other needs and has the skill and self-confidence to make their own fashion statements, or in the 'consumer with a conscience' who would only buy garments and products they know are 'green' or eco-friendly, not cruel to animals or made and sold under 'Fair Trade' arrangements. Interestingly, in terms

The Body Shop: successfully marketing to the 'consumer with a conscience' as well as campaigning on environmental issues.

of fashion, the most fundamental physiological needs and the highest self-actualization needs can both be fulfilled by charity store clothing!

It is important to note, however, that our needs – like our age, income, place of work and residence, our family and, of course, our body – change over time, and changes in our lives are also accompanied by changes in motivation towards fashion purchasing. It is also likely that many motives for buying fashion may be operating at the same time: one motive (perhaps the need for status and esteem) may make us 'positive' towards a garment or product, while at the same time we may be 'negative' towards the same garment or product because it is simply not warm enough. Yet, we are often unable or even unwilling to admit to some of the motives that move us to buy certain garments. In fact, we will often lie to ourselves and to others about why we bought something! We may assert to ourselves and our friends that we bought a garment because it looked nice rather than because we thought it would impress them. Consequently, because of the fickleness of human nature itself, measuring consumer motivation is problematic.

OTHER PSYCHOLOGICAL APPROACHES

The problem that faces marketers is that consumers are each unique personalities. Early approaches to understanding consumer behaviour concentrated on personality traits and tried to discover 'consumer types'. The hope was that once marketers had identified certain types of consumers, their behaviour could be predicted and fashion products could be produced and promoted in the appropriate manner for those 'types'. Unfortunately, it turned out that there was very little correlation between personality types and buying behaviour!

A second approach was based not on personality traits but on AIOs (Activities, Interests and Opinions). Consumers are asked questions ranging from the general to the specific. Usually based on the Lickert Scale, respondents are asked to indicate their level of agreement or disagreement about a product or subject, ranging from 'Strongly Agree' to 'Strongly Disagree' with 'Don't Know/Neutral' in the middle and with scores allocated to each response. Lickert Scales are popular in marketing because as well as being relatively easy to construct, they also give fairly accurate information about the degree of a respondent's feelings. The data is then analysed alongside demographic and purchasing data about consumers to 'create' distinct groups who have AIOs in common.

Another area of consumer personality study concentrates on the analysis of 'self-concept'. For fashion marketers this approach seems to offer promise, since clothing is itself the most visible way in which we express ourselves. The area of 'self-concept' includes:

- the *self-image* – how we see ourselves

- the *ideal self-image* – how we would like to see ourselves

- the *social self-image* – how we think other people see us

- the *ideal social self-image* – how we would like other people to see us

We buy clothing both to maintain and enhance our self-image, but our self image is affected by many factors, including age and social class.

The underlying question that marketers are seeking to answer is whether buying is a rational or emotional process. For the fashion marketer, our rational decisions as consumers are those based on objective criteria such as size, price and convenience. Our emotional motives are subjective: our purchases are based on our need for esteem or status. While it could be argued that when we shop for clothing we are 'rational' and when we shop for fashion we are 'emotional', it is more likely that we bring a mixture of rational and emotional factors out shopping with us, and part of fashion marketing's remit is to try to understand the 'emotional driving forces' and the 'rational constraints' involved in buying fashion items.

Age plays an important role in determining what we buy and where we buy it. Our self concept is expressed through our clothing and, during the teen years, this may well be at odds with the concepts of those who have to pay for our fashions – namely our parents!

THE RAW MATERIALS

Producing any goods requires raw materials, and in the case of fashion these are textiles, pelts and skins – known collectively as the 'primary markets'. Textiles is by far the largest of these three industries: in the USA alone the textile industry directly employs over 500,000 people who produce a wholesale output worth around £44 billion (c. $70 billion) a year.

SYNTHETIC FIBRES

The arrival of man-made fibres more than fifty years ago not only introduced new fabrics with amazing properties like 'drip-dry' and 'permanent press', it also revolutionized the textile industry's marketing activities. In the past, marketing by natural-fibre producers (the cotton, linen, wool and silk producers) was relatively simple. A crop (or herd) was raised, it was harvested (or sheared) and the fibres sold at local markets to wholesalers who sold the fibre on at central markets. Farmers and growers were therefore largely unconcerned with fabric construction or garment production. In little over half a century, the industry has shifted from being dominated by natural fibres to one where synthetic-fibre production accounts for an

estimated 60 per cent of the world market.

The man-made fibre industry developed out of early attempts to make 'artificial silk'. The beauty, scarcity and cost of natural silk made it the first-choice fibre in the search for a man-made alternative, and the first artificial silk was produced in the late 1880s. The apparent ease with which the larva of the Chinese silkworm moth (*Bombyx mori*) transforms the cellulose from the mulberry leaves on which it feeds into a protein gum which hardens after extrusion into a single silken filament disguises a complex chemical process which even today cannot be exactly duplicated in the laboratory. Commercial farming of silkworms today – where the poor silkworms are asphyxiated in their cocoons once they have produced their valuable thread – accounts for 85 per cent of world silk production. The remaining 15 per cent is provided by 'wild silk', where the moths are allowed to leave their cocoons before harvesting.

While the textile industry continued with its experiments to improve on artificial silk, it was eventually realized that a more successful future lay in the development of artificial textile fibres in their own right, and not as inferior copies of natural fibres. In the 1920s the term 'rayon' was

Silk filament being weighed in a Florentine textile mill. Silk filaments are obtained by unwinding the cocoons – a delicate and highly-skilled operation. Although a cocoon may contain some 3000m of silk filament, there can be as little as 1000m of 'first quality' material. The waste filament is converted into spun silk.

used to identify man-made staple fibres – fibres cut into designated staple lengths. With the general interest in rayon, the man-made textile industry was born.

Today there are three main categories of man-made fibres:

REGENERATED FIBRES are made from natural fibre-forming filaments such as cellulose derived from wood pulp, cotton linters and other vegetable matter and certain protein materials (including protein derived from maize, peanuts, soya beans and milk) which are chemically shaped and made into filaments. The regenerated fibres are: *viscose* (the modern form of the earliest type of artificial silk), *cuprammonium* (which until nylon came along was considered the best substitute for silk in lingerie and hosiery and is today used for dress fabrics under names such as Bemberg and Cuprama), *acetate* (first produced in 1921 and still considered a better artificial silk than viscose, and also less expensive to produce) and *triacetate* (a fibre developed as early as 1914 but which only became available in the 1950s, used primarily for the production of permanently pleated fabrics).

SYNTHETIC FIBRES are made from substances not normally thought of as fibrous or which do not form fibres in nature, such as coal and

The natural beauty, scarcity and cost of silk made it the first choice in the development of a manmade alternative.

petroleum. The main types of synthetic fibres in clothing use are various types of *nylons* (polyamides or long-chain polymers discovered by a team led by Dr Wallace Carruthers at the American company Du Pont in 1928), *polyesters* (brand names include Trevira, Terylene and Dacron), *acrylics* (such as Orlon, most commonly used in knitwear), *modacrylics* (like Dynel, used for fur fabrics, and Teklan for warm-textured nightwear), *elastenes* (the Spandex and Lycra stretch fabrics), *polypropylenes* (used in knitted fabrics for sports and thermal clothing), *chlorofibres* (such as Rhovyl used for thermal wear – its soft, fleecy quality also makes it popular for sportswear) and *aramids* (high-strength fibres like Kevlar and

Nomex, first used in protective clothing designed for fighter pilots and later used in the space suits for the Apollo missions).

MISCELLANEOUS TYPES include fibres made from substances like metal and glass. Metal filaments – gold and silver thread – are probably the oldest man-made textile materials, but today modern metallic filaments like Lurex, based on coloured aluminium foil, mean that we can sparkle on a budget!

The latest in fabric technology: Stowaway Active, Resort and Street 'compact fashions', designed by Rosemary Moore to fit into a handbag, are made from a woven mixture of Lycra and nylon.

free spirit *travel light*

pack

The impact on the textile industry

The development of man-made fibres has transformed the textile industry from a highly fragmented, highly specialized operation into an industry dominated by international giants. While chemical companies like Du Pont, ICI, Monsato, Eastman Kodak and Phillips Petroleum dominate the fibre-production market, a handful of companies, including Milliken and Guilford Mills, operate vertically integrated businesses: they process the fibres, spin the yarns, make the cloth and finish it (using processes like dyeing, printing, waterproofing, etc.). With sales in excess of £2 billion ($3.2 billion), Burlington Industries is one of the world's largest producers of textiles and related goods and does everything from researching and developing new fibres to the production of finished fabrics, as well as manufacturing its own branded products (Burlington Hosiery and Burlington Sock) and marketing its own products via licensing agreements with companies like Anne Klein, Oleg Cassini and Levi Strauss.

These developments have meant that the whole structure of the textiles industry has changed, moving from manufacturing-oriented to marketing-oriented, responding to market or customer needs, with an emphasis on the ultimate consumer – the man and woman in the stores. This is also sometimes known as changing from a 'push system'(where products are 'pushed' onto customers) to a 'pull system' (where information about customers and their preferences is 'pulled' in by market research and then the things people want are made). This situation contrasts with previous decades when the textile industry's targets for promotion and sales were the intermediary companies who purchased their fibres, yarns and goods. Consequently, until the late 1950s most ordinary shoppers did not know the difference between one brand name fibre and another. In order to gain the consumer's confidence and acceptance of new fibres and fabrics, the large chemical and textile companies began the aggressive advertising campaigns which continue today and which are directed at the ultimate consumers of their goods.

While many early adverts focused on the new 'wonder' features of the fibres and concentrated on brand recognition, other adverts were, and continue to be, made in co-operation with apparel manufacturers to show both the virtues of the fibre and fabrics as well as fashionable garments themselves, thereby creating demand and new markets.

In addition to advertising fibres on an individual basis – such as the recent 'Lycra by Du Pont' advertising – fibre promotion is also carried our collectively by groups such as the Man-Made Fibres Producers Association, an organization whose aim is to inform consumers about fibres regardless of the company that produces them. Under this association's watchful eye, other associations operate: the Polyester Fashion Council, an alliance of six US polyester producers – American Enka, American Hoechst,

Marks and Spencer and Lycra by Du Pont: collaborative promotions between textile producers and apparel manufacturers demonstrate the virtues of the new fibres as well as new fashion statements.

Technical data about a fibre's properties does not generally move retail consumers to purchase. Lycra by Du Pont's campaign to increase awareness was achieved by showing consumers the vast range of garments in which Lycra could be used.

Avtex Fibers, Celanese Fibers, Eastman Chemical and E.I. Du Pont Nemours – was largely responsible for revising the contemporary mind set of a world that associated polyester with shiny suits and bad taste. Through innovative fashion presentations to retail trade associations, the council has successfully transformed the Cinderella of the fibre world into a fashionable princess.

NATURAL FIBRES

Natural fibre producers, because of their relatively small size, also have their trade associations who compile and disseminate fibre and fabric information to their members and to consumers. One such organization is the intenational research, development and marketing company behind the Woolmark. Founded in 1937 as the International Wool Secretariat, the institution is funded by woolgrowers in Australia and exists to optimize their profitablility by building and sustaining global demand for their wools. The Woolmark organization has 20 branches around the world and representation in 60 countries.

Launched in 1964, the Woolmark was designed to identify Pure New Wool products and to signify quality and reliability. Only companies who agree to meet strict production and performance control standards can qualify to be licensed and use the mark on their products.

In 1971 the Woolblendmark was introduced to identify products made from wool blended with other fibres. As with the Woolmark, manufacturers from spinners through to makers-up must hold a licence in order to use the Woolblendmark and their products must meet stringent quality standards. In order to carry the

Woolblendmark, natural fibre blends must contain a minimum of 50 per cent wool; in blends of wool and man-made fibre the finished product must contain a minimum of 60 per cent wool. The use of the marks is strictly controlled and internationally monitored.

Actively engaged in research and development, the organization has an increasingly commercial focus and is a leading source of international textile market information. It provides yarn, fabric and garment sourcing services to industry and retail and is engaged in the energetic promotion of Woolmark and Woolblendmark products and a range of specialized sub-brands across the world.

Similar activities in advertising, merchandising, publicicity, market research and fashion marketing are undertaken by offices like Cotton Incorporated in the USA (a branch of the Cotton Institute) and the International Linen Promotion Commission – the US arm of the International Linen Federation, a Paris-based organization which includes flax-growers from Continental Europe, Japan and the UK (including Northern Ireland and Scotland).

Each of these trade organizations also maintains extensive libraries of fabrics in the major fashion centres like London, Paris and New York. Many of the large fibre-producers also maintain libraries of samples from every mill or converter (a textile producer that buys in greige goods – unbleached, unfinished fabrics – from the mills and then dyes, prints and finishes fabrics before selling them on to apparel manufacturers). These libraries are a valuable tool for designers since they give an overall picture of what fabrics are available and if a specific fabric is required, the library can help locate the mill or converter who created it. The Cotton Incorporated library also has a CAD (computer-aided design) system which allows designers to scan in samples of fabrics and work with them on a computer screen in different colour, pattern and silhouette schemes.

In addition to advertising, the textile producers also undertake numerous other marketing activities including consumer education and protection, providing technical advice, carrying out research and development, and staging presentations and trade shows.

LABELLING AND LEGISLATION

In terms of labelling, standards for consumer information and protection are largely government-imposed. In the UK, in accordance with EU directives, composition labelling (where the predominant fibre in a textile is listed first with its content percentage, then any other fibres in decreasing order of their percentage) is compulsory by law. Furthermore, it is the responsibility of the manufacturer to specify the content percentages under their correct EU generic names, although it is the retailer's responsibility to ensure that any garments made from the fabric are correctly labelled.

In the USA in 1954, the Flammable Fabrics Act banned certain fabrics from the American market. In 1973 the Federal Trade Commission (FTC) amended the Act, and certain categories of clothing (such as children's wear and night attire) had to comply with new US Government standards regarding flammability. In the UK, textile manufacturers must tread carefully when they make claims for special fabric properties such as 'flame retardant' since the 1987 Consumer Protection Act places the liability for defective products on them, without consumers having to prove negligence. Another federal act in the USA, the Care Labelling of Wearing Apparel Act, was also passed by the FTC, under which manufacturers are required to provide specific guidance regarding the washing and/or dry cleaning methods to be used by consumers.

In the UK, the Home Laundering Consultation Council (HLCC) evolved a system of care labelling some years ago in which a series of recommended methods was numbered 1–9, with the emphasis on home laundering. Today a system of 11 basic labels informs the consumer about the recommended temperature of the wash water. A bar underneath the diagram of a wash tub recommends a gentler machine action, and a broken or double bar indicates 'Woolwash' at 40°C (104°F). Articles which cannot be washed by any procedures come under the eleventh label type, 'Do Not Wash'. Now covered by the British Standard Code of Practice for Textile Care

Labelling (BS 2747:1986), the design and information content of the labels was agreed upon by representatives drawn from the textile industry, manufacturers of domestic appliances, household soaps and detergents and consumer groups.

Fibre companies invest a great deal of time and money in the research and development of new fibre variants: it can take as long as fifteen years between development of a new fibre and the appearance of a fabric made from that fibre in a retail store. This in part explains why many fibre companies are often researching and developing similar fibres at the same time. For example, the form of anti-shrink treatment used for producing Woolmark knitted wool garments was developed by wool research organizations linked to the International Wool Secretariat, but similar processes involving an initial chlorine-based treatment followed by application of a fine synthetic polymer coating to the fibres were also being developed by individual companies.

ENVIRONMENTAL CONCERNS

Acknowledging the increased consumer awareness of global environmental and ethical issues and the new demand for eco-friendly

Care diagrams agreed by the textile industry, consumer groups and manufacturers of domestic appliances and detergents as part of the British Standard Code of Practice for Textile Care Labelling.

While many textile companies invest heavily in research and the development of new fibre variants, their innovations are balanced by tradition. This Florentine silk weavers continues to use machinery first made in the seventeenth century.

products, the textile industry is not only researching and developing 'green' textiles but new methods of operation that are non-polluting and resource-efficient. Rather than printing a surface pattern onto a textile, the Nuno Corporation in Tokyo uses traditional jacquard weaving techniques to incorporate design into the weave. The fabrics designed for Nuno by Junichi Arai, while intended for mass production, make extensive use of undyed, unbleached fibres to create innovative and fashionable fabrics that are also environmentally friendly.

In an effort to produce a 'green cotton', the Danish textile manufacturer Novotex have invested in an organic cotton plantation, and rather than use chemical processes to produce knitted cotton fabrics, mechanical treatments and bleaching using hydrogen peroxide (rather than the potentially more hazardous chlorine) are used. Fabrics are dyed using natural dyes wherever possible in a closed-jet system to minimize water consumption, and the water used is then purified to minimize the risk of residue discharged into the environment.

COLOUR TRENDS

The difference between a saleable fabric and a market failure lies not only in fibre properties but in colour, and the long-range planning of the textile industry involves colour development. Twice a year in Paris, members of the International Colour Authority meet. An association of representatives from fibre companies and colour services, the ICA analyses colour direction two years in advance of the target selling season. Twenty months before the selling season starts, in March and September the ICA sends out its colour predictions to the world-wide fashion industry. The ICA assists dyers, spinners and weavers (both industrial concerns and individual 'craftsman-producers') as well as apparel manufacturers to make long-term colour decisions. Their reports provide samples of key colours in the form of twists of yarn and cover clothing as well as home furnishings, and they include an explanatory text in three languages.

Since 1915 the Color Association of the United States (CAUS) has helped American fashion businesses make the right colour choices. It provides swatched colour forecasts for women's, men's and children's fashions specifically for the US market. Also geared specifically to this market is the colour forecast provided by The Color Box. In addition to colour swatches, The Color Box also provides the fashion industry with information on which colours are suited to particular target segments of the American fashion market. Not only do the textile producers, the fashion designers and the clothing manufacturers find this information valuable when planning new lines, it is also of great interest to accessory and shoe designers and manufacturers, who will co-ordinate their range according to the colour predictions, and to retailers, who may well want to alter the appearance of their stores – they may even have to consider different in-store lighting strategies in order to allow customers to see the 'true colours' of garments. Furthermore, the cosmetic industry will develop ranges of colours and tones to complement the coming season's colour trends.

FABRIC SHOWS

In addition to fashion shows staged to launch a new fibre or fabric concept, twice a year important fabric shows are held in Europe to showcase new fabrics, new colours and new patterns to apparel manufacturers.

Premier Vision is held in Paris in March and October and is the earliest source for fashion fabrics. In April and October or early November, designers, buyers and the press gather in Frankfurt, Germany, for Interstoff, to view the complete lines of over a thousand exhibitors. Immediately after Interstoff comes IdeaComo, primarily an exhibition of the latest designs in Italian silks and the source of many *haute couture* fabrics. In December and June in Paris – much closer to the actual selling season – Nouvelles Rencontres ('New Meetings') is held, organized to appeal to 'private label' manufacturers who make apparel for the large department stores or chain stores who wish to sell garments under their own brand name or private label.

While American textile producers show their wares in Europe, there are also fabric shows in New York and Los Angeles where fabric lines are presented four times a year to coincide with the American fashion seasons of Fall I, Fall II, Summer, Resort and Spring.

INTERNATIONAL COMPETITION

Because of low production costs, the European and American textile industries have faced increased competition from Asian and Pacific Rim producers, as well as more recently from former Eastern Bloc countries like Romania, and in their efforts to fight cheaper imports, the textile industries in the West have been forced to devise new marketing strategies to meet consumer demand, adopt new technologies and develop international trade agreements.

In the USA, textile producers formed the Crafted with Pride in the USA Council to promote American-made goods, and to beat imported products in the race to the consumer, a computer strategy called 'Quick Response' (QR) has been developed to reduce waiting time in ordering and distribution between textile manufacturers, garment producers and retailers. It is now possible to ally all the levels of the fashion industry via Electronic Data Interchange (EDI) since all goods are given a Universal Product Code (UPC) – a bar code which identifies the style, colour, size, fabrication and vendor. Now when fast-selling items leave the shop, the bar-coded information is laser-scanned and fed through EDI to manufacturers (who will cut new stock) and to textile producers (who will provide new fabric in the correct colourway to the manufacturers). In the UK, the Just In Time (JIT) inventory control system offers a similar system to QR.

Trade regulations

In 1974, as a temporary framework for regulating the international trade in fibres, fabrics and clothing between the developing 'low-cost production' countries and the industrialized 'First World' producers, the Multi Fibre Agreement (MFA) regulated trade in textiles and apparel of cotton, wool and man-made fibres through bilaterally agreed quotas which were scrutinized and revised in order to meet continually changing economic circumstances world-wide. As part of the Uruguay Round of GATT (General Agreement on Tariffs and Trade) it was decided that the MFA would be phased out over a ten-year period from 1994.

Many European and American textile producers and clothing manufacturers are concerned that the demise of the MFA will result in increased low-cost imports of clothing and textiles from abroad. It is hoped that in place of the MFA, GATT agreements being negotiated at this time will cover issues such as dumping, industry subsidies and the counterfeiting of design: the cheap mass production of fake or designer-name copies is a growing industry and an increasing cause for concern to designers and manufacturers.

Because fashion is international and many of the major synthetic-fibre producers and textile giants are multinational companies, trade agreements such as GATT will play an increasingly important role in each sector of the fashion industry's marketing strategies for the future.

MARKETING METHODS

Like the word 'fashion', the word 'market' has many different though related meanings. It often refers to the potential demand for a product, therefore the market is made up of consumers. Manufacturers must know whether there is a demand for their products as well as be able to develop new products that meet new consumer demands. A market is also a physical space. On the one hand it is the place where the buyers and the sellers of fashion meet to conduct their business – in showrooms or at apparel marts for wholesale fashions, and in stores for retail fashions.

At the retail end of the fashion market there have been several new developments whereby the customer need no longer 'go to market' but the market comes to them in the form of mail-order catalogues and televised home shopping. On the other hand, 'market' can also refer to an area – such as the domestic market or the international market – and while it is possible to buy and sell fashion all year round, 'market' also means the specific times of the year when weeks have been scheduled for the release of new collections and lines.

While the terms 'collection opening' and 'line release' both mean the first opportunity to see

Catwalk extravaganzas are the most important tool in presenting *haute couture* and *prêt-à-porter* to the retail buyers and the press.

new fashion merchandise, 'collection opening' refers specifically to the shows staged by the major European fashion houses, while 'line release' refers to the launching of the new season's lines by other manufacturers.

After each collection or line is designed, it must be presented to retail-store buyers so that they can purchase it for their store's stock. The presentations used vary from the catwalk extravaganzas of *haute couture* and designer *prêt-à-porter* to trade fairs and individual demonstrations by sales representatives who sell to the smaller, independent stores.

THE EUROPEAN MARKET

In Europe, the *couture* collection openings take place twice a year. In Paris, the twenty-five or so *couture* houses show their spring/summer collections in January, whereas fall/winter collections are presented in July. While these Paris shows – particularly those by the 'famous name' houses like Dior, Chanel, Yves Saint Laurent and Givenchy – may attract the most attention, it is worth remembering that Italy,

Skiwear by Giorgio Armani. Armani is one of the best-known names of Italian *moda pronta*. Fashion is now the second largest industry in Italy and the country is the world's largest exporter of clothing.

England and Spain also have a *couture* industry although on a much smaller scale.

In Italy, fashion is the second largest industry after tourism, and the country has become the world's largest exporter of clothing, including knitwear, menswear and shoes. While the Italian fashion industry is devoted mainly to *moda pronta* ('ready-to-wear') which is based in Milan, limited *alta-moda* (*couture*) remains in Rome and is governed by the *Camera Nazionale dell'Alta Moda Italiana* (National Chamber of Italian Couture) which operates in a similar regulatory manner to the French *Chambre Syndicale* and whose most well-known members include Raffael Curiel, André Laug, Milan Schon, Irene Galitzine, Odicini, Carlo Tivoli and, of course, Valentino (Valentino Gavarani – not to be confused with the *moda-pronta* designer Mario Valentino). Many of the Italian *moda-pronta* designers have added *alta-moda* arms to their businesses: Gianfranco Ferre has designed *couture* for the house of Dior, and the late Gianni Versace launched a *couture* collection for both men and women called 'Atelier Versace'.

Made-to-measure in Britain: now largely confined to bespoke gentlemen's outfitters like Henry Poole and Co.

The late Patrick Kelly, the first American designer to be awarded *createur* status by the *Chambre Syndicale*.

Italian *alta-moda* collections are traditionally shown just before the Paris *couture* shows to allow time for customers to travel between them. Spain also has *couture* shows twice a year under the aegis of the Alta Costura, which showcases the work of designers like Carmen Mir, Pertegaz and Pedro Rovira, while in England, though most of the *couture* houses have gone, the two names that remain synonymous with British *couture* are Norman Hartnell and Hardy Amies, both of whom had long-standing relationships with the Queen and the royal family. 'Made-to-measure' clothing in Britain is now largely associated with the bespoke (custom tailoring) outfitters of Savile Row, establishments like Gieves and Hawkes, H. Huntsman and Sons, Kilgour Weatherill, Anderson and Sheppard, Turnbull and Asser and, of course, the oldest established

MARKETING METHODS

Savile Row firm of Henry Poole.

As in other countries, most French fashion is mass-produced. yet ironically, the top-of-the-range designer-name *prêt-à-porter* is not inexpensive: prices can be as high as £2,500 ($4,000) for a single garment, even though it is standard size and sold 'off the rack'. Only the price tag confers a degree of exclusivity.

In France in 1975, in recognition of the role played by *prêt-à-porter* fashion, the *Chambre Syndicale de la Fédération Française de la Couture* formed the *Chambre Syndicale du Prêt-à-Porter des Couturiers et des Createurs de la Mode*, which was organized by Yves Saint Laurent's business partner, Pierre Bergé. Of the 44 members, 24 are '*Createurs*' – designers who work exclusively in *prêt-à-porter* such as Jean Paul Gaultier and Sonia Rykiel – with the remaining 20 members, including Dior, Cardin and Courrèges, producing both *haute couture* and *prêt-à-porter* collections. Not all the designers on the createur list are French: Japanese designers Kenzo and Yohji Yamamoto are members and in 1988, Patrick Kelly of Mississippi was the first American to be accorded *createur* status. Tragically, Kelly's career was cut short with his death two years later. Today, as American ready-to-wear design grows in international popularity, in addition to their US line releases, many American designers are also showing in Paris.

The *Chambre Syndicale du Prêt-à-Porter* schedules and co-ordinates the openings of the *prêt* collections in March and October of each year at the Forum des Halles and at the Louvre

Of the 44 members of the *Chambre Syndicale*, 24 are designated *createurs*, working exclusively in ready-to-wear. Not all are French: leading Japanese designer Yohji Yamamoto has been a member since 1988.

Museum. At the same time as the designer *prêt* shows are happening, more than a thousand French apparel manufacturers – companies like Naf Naf and Girbaud – are staging an exhibition called the *Salon du Prêt-à-Porter Féminine* at the Porte de Versailles. These manufacturers of ready-to-wear are not represented by the *Chambre Syndicale* but by their own association, the *Fédération Française du Prêt-à-Porter Féminine* which organizes the shows and co-ordinates the industry's activities.

Both the *Fédération Française de la Couture*

(which oversees the functions of the various *Chambres Syndicales*) and the *Fédération Française du Prêt-à-Porter Féminine* primarily focus their promotion and marketing activities within the domestic market. Marketing French fashions abroad is the role of the government-formed trade association, the *Fédération Française des Industries de l'Habillement*. In their efforts to encourage the rest of the world to consume more French fashion, the federation sponsors the participation of French designers at international trade shows in Germany, Italy, and Japan and also maintains a permanent New York office called the French Fashion and Textile Center.

Although Italian styling and fashion in menswear became popular in the rest of Europe – in particular in Britain – in the 1950s and 1960s, it was not until the 1970s that Italian women's *moda-pronta* became organized and centred on Milan, close to the fabric sources at Como, Biella and Turin. Here the *Associazione Italiana Industriali Abbligiamento et Moglieria* (Italian Fashion Industry Association) organizes and schedules the *Milanovendamoda* (Milan ready-to-wear) show which coincides with the designer ready-to-wear collection shows under the auspices of the *Camera Nazionale della Moda Italiana* (National Chamber of Italian Fashion). Carefully planned, the Milan shows 'jump the gun' on France with their collections and lines just a week before the Paris shows!

The London shows traditionally follow Paris, when London Fashion Week stages the British Designer Shows and the London Designer Collections. Despite all the razzmatazz of the often very theatrical shows and all the accompanying international media attention, neither Milan, Paris nor London is the largest fashion market – that honour goes to the German fashion fair IGEDO (*Interessensgemeinschaft für Damenoberkleidung* – literally translated as the equally impressive 'Community of Interest for Women's Outer Garments'!). Here, manufacturers from over seventy countries show their lines to nearly a quarter of a million buyers twice a year in March and October.

However, the fashion market is not just about womenswear, and during the year new menswear and children's wear collections and lines are presented. In France, a third arm of the *Chambre Syndicale*, the *Chambre Syndicale de la Mode Masculine*, organizes the twice-yearly menswear shows in the *Salon d'Habillement Masculine* (SEHM) in Paris each February and September, featuring the collections of the leading European menswear designers. The same months see the new lines in children's wear at the *Salon de la Mode Enfantine*.

In Italy, in addition to the Milan shows by the *Milanovendamoda Uomo* ('Designer Men's Ready-to-wear from Milan'), in Florence in January and June there are the *Pitti Uomo* and *Uomo Italia* shows of menswear as well as the *Pitti Bimbo* and *Moda Bimbo* children's wear shows. Meanwhile, London plays host to IMBEX (the International Men's and Boy's Wear Exhibition) and Cologne in Germany is the location for the *Herren-Mode-Woche* ('Menswear Week').

AMERICAN MARKETING

The American fashion market operates in a slightly different way to its European counterparts. In the USA, line releases for 'better quality' ready-to-wear usually occur not twice a year but a staggering five times a year: January for Summer; February/March for the Fall I season; March/April for the main Fall II season and Holiday lines; August is the release month for Resort Wear and October/November sees the launch of fashions for Spring.

At the heart of the American fashion industry is the production of women's wear, which accounts for around two-thirds of all clothing made and which generates an estimated £1.25 billion ($2 billion) worth of trade each year. Of the 3,000 or so businesses engaged in the production of women's wear in America, most are located in the eastern seaboard states – particularly, Pennsylvania, New Jersey and New

A famous brand name in sportswear and swimwear, Jantzen is part of the giant VF Corporation which also markets Lee and Wrangler jeanswear.

York. New York City itself is home to nearly 70 per cent of the entire country's annual women's wear production, however, and the apparel industry is the city's primary private employer.

In a relatively small area of mid-town Manhattan – the fashion capital of the USA – are the headquarters and showrooms of nearly every apparel manufacturer in the country, although increasingly, garment construction is shifting to other states, with some companies like Calvin Klein moving all their manufacturing out of the USA completely to the Pacific Rim.

While the majority of women's wear companies in America are small, privately owned businesses, there is a minority of giants like the VF Corporation, which has four divisions producing a wide range of apparel. In addition to Vanity Fair Intimate Apparel, the VF Corporation also markets Lee and Wrangler jeanswear as well as Jantzen sportswear. Some of the other giants on the American fashion scene include Levi Strauss, Murjani International (which first came to public attention in the 'designer denim wars' of the 1970s) and one of the wonder companies of the 1980s, Liz Claiborne. Formed in 1976 in partnership with her husband, Arthur Ortenberg, Claiborne rapidly built the largest and most profitable women's wear company in the world with no less than 13 separate divisions, including their own retail stores. Now vertically integrated, Liz Claiborne takes care of the design, manufacture, distribution and retailing of women's and men's fashions – the entire process 'from sheep to shop'!

Designs such as these from Liz Claiborne underpin a vertically integrated fashion empire that is also the most profitable women's wear company in the world.

Apart from a few individuals (notably Arnold Scassi, who has consistently maintained a reputation for fine, made-to-measure evening wear), the USA does not really have an equivalent to the European *haute couture*

industry. However, there are highly original designers like Donna Karan, Galanos, Bill Blass, Oscar de la Renta, Calvin Klein and Ralph Lauren who do produce high-quality, high-fashion merchandise. As leaders in the industry, the creations designed by such famous names are often referred to as 'couture-ready-to-wear'.

Brand names vs designer names

Because of the dominance in American menswear of large corporations, menswear in the USA has traditionally been marketed with an emphasis on manufacturer's brand names rather than designer names. Old established American menswear labels like Arrow, Fruit of the Loom, Levi Strauss and Lee have been joined by newer brands like Nike, Reebok and Dockers. Nevertheless, since the 1970s designer-name menswear has been making inroads in American men's fashions, first from European designers like Pierre Cardin, Nino Cerutti, Giorgio Armani and Hugo Boss and then from home-grown talents like Ralph Lauren, Calvin Klein, Geoffrey Beene, Bill Blass, Donna Karan and Oscar de la Renta.

While there has been an increased interest in menswear in the last thirty years or so, in the USA trade groups and associations have been hard at work promoting and marketing American menswear for much longer. One of the oldest American associations is the Clothing Manufacturers Association (CMA), which represents manufacturers of tailored clothing and co-ordinates and presents new styling trends to its members. In 1953, to help market a brand

new line of menswear, the National Association of Men's Sportswear Buyers (NAMSB) was created. Four times a year, in January, March, June and October, NAMSB stages the world's largest menswear trade show in New York, where over a thousand manufacturers show 37 categories of apparel to around 30,000 retail store buyers.

Meanwhile, the Designer's Collective, established in 1979, serves to showcase designer-label tailored clothing, sportswear, outwear, separates and accessories and is sponsored by the American menswear industry's public relations organization, the Men's Fashion Association (MFA), which in association with the makers of Cutty Sark Scotch has created the Cutty Sark Men's Fashion Awards for to those designers who have made outstanding contributions to the field of men's fashions.

CUTTING OUT THE MIDDLEMEN

In addition to the large fashion shows, other channels of distribution exist for getting fashion from the manufacturers to the stores. For instance, wholesalers can also be manufacturers – such as Jeffrey Rogers – who manufacture and sell wholesale under their own label. While wholesalers remain useful to small, independent or privately owned retail stores because they will 'break bulk' (sell in small quantities, though often with a minimum order value), increasingly, the

UK mass merchandiser Marks and Spencer was among the first retailers to deal direct with manufacturers, giving it control over product quality and, often, exclusivity in design.

large multiples and department stores are dealing direct with suppliers through their centralized buying offices. Consequently, they are able to avoid the middlemen wholesalers and the associated costs, as wholesalers which buy in bulk from manufacturers need to cover their buying and storing costs by 'marking up' or adding a percentage to the original cost price. The increased price must be borne by the retailers, who will inevitably pass it on to their customers.

In the UK, Marks & Spencers was one of the first retailers to deal direct with manufacturers. In addition to the financial benefits, Marks & Spencers have found they have increased control over product quality, and exclusive deals struck with manufacturers allow them to retail garments that are 'different' in design, fabrication or colour to those stocked by their competitors.

Other wholesalers may operate as importers or agents (or sales representatives). Rather than having to bear the expense of overseas buying trips, retail store buyers can use importers which often offer specialist merchandise such as silks from the Far East, 'ethnic clothing' such as saris or woven woollen garments from Central and South America, or accessories and jewellery. Unlike importers, agents do not hold stock but have only samples of merchandise, either from the company that directly employs them (Levi Strauss employs agents to sell to smaller outlets) or samples of merchandise from non-competing lines. As well as having showrooms, agents will also travel to retailers, but like sales representatives, agents' operations may be limited to a particular geographical area.

DISTRIBUTION POLICIES

In order to attract target customers and therefore certain types of retail stores, manufacturers have to plan their distribution to ensure that the 'right' stores buy their merchandise, that their merchandise is represented in the right geographical areas, that one retailer does not create unfair competition for another, and finally, that enough stock is turned over in order to create a profit. In order to achieve these aims, manufacturers can operate a number of distribution policies.

An *open distribution* policy is one where a manufacturer will sell to anyone who can pay for their goods.

A *selected distribution* policy, on the other hand, limits the number or type of stores that can buy a line or collection. The national chain of drug stores in Britain, Superdrug, successfully challenged the manufacturers of designer-name fragrances – in particular Chanel – when it decided to stock the fragrance and sell it for less than major department stores. Chanel believed that the cachet of designer-exclusivity that came with their name was being compromised by the more 'downmarket' retail practice of Superdrug. A compromise was reached when Superdrug agreed to limit the number of outlets selling this and other 'fine fragrances' and to install special display units and sales counters in their stores dedicated to the sales of designer perfumes. Most recently in Britain, Adidas, the giant manufacturer of top-of-the-range sportswear, did battle with supermarket giant Tesco in an effort to stop the store from selling its products. While Adidas did not object to Tesco selling their goods, they were outraged at the supermarket's policy of undercutting the much higher 'high street' prices which were being charged by other Adidas retailers.

Exclusive distribution policies are common in the menswear industry in the USA (manufacturers sell their goods exclusively through their own retail outlets), while in a *dual distribution* system manufacturers sell their goods through their own manufacturer-owned retail stores as well as selling their merchandise wholesale to independent retailers. Dual distribution policies are largely confined to a very few large and well-known manufacturers like Botany Industries, Phillips-Van Heusen, Ralph Lauren, Calvin Klein, Donna Karan, Giorgio Armani and the giant Hartmax Corporation which owns 468 retail stores and produces 32 'manufacturer brands' and licensed-label merchandise (including Austin Reed, Nino Cerutti and parts of the Christian Dior and Pierre Cardin menswear range) sold to company-owned stores and independent stores in America.

FRANCHISING

An increasingly popular method of conducting overseas business is franchising, defined by the International Franchise Association as a contractual relationship between a franchisee who, for a fee or royalty, sells the franchiser's (producer's) merchandise. The franchiser is obliged to maintain a continuing interest in the franchisee in the areas of training and product knowledge, while the franchisee must maintain the reputation of the name and image of the franchiser.

There are advantages to both parties: the franchisee usually benefits because the name is usually well known and the 'parent company' has generally made inroads into the market. Furthermore, all the advertising of the 'name' is undertaken nationally (and in some cases, internationally) by the franchiser. For the franchiser, they can distribute their products nationally or internationally without having the expense of operating and staffing the retail outlets themselves.

Some of the most well-known 'franchised fashions' are French Connection, Mondi,

Stefanel, The Tie Rack, Joseph Tricot, The Body Shop, Estée Lauder cosmetics (which are franchised to department stores) and Benetton – despite the company's claims that they do not franchise!

LICENSING

As a method of conducting business internationally, licensing is closely linked to franchising. Licensing involves a company selling the use of some of its assets – the designer's name, the actual designs or the company logo – to other companies. Ralph Lauren now licenses his name and logo to a range of products, including bags, belts and sunglasses. The extent of Lauren's licensing operations means that his company now owns only one factory making tailored menswear and two flagship stores in New York: all the other products that bear the Ralph Lauren name or Polo logo and all the 125 Ralph Lauren-Polo boutiques world-wide are under license from the designer.

Used with care, licensing can be an excellent source of revenue for a company, but the task of maintaining balance between profiting from the prestige of their name and potentially damaging a company's image or reputation through overexposure is not easy. The simple overuse of a designer's name can devalue it, and this is exactly what happened to Pierre Cardin in the 1980s – over 800 licensees meant that in some instances, poor quality merchandise was being marketed under the Pierre Cardin label, and granting licenses for everything from ties, perfumes, hosiery and sunglasses to scuba diving suits,

The King of Licensing, Pierre Cardin. In the 1980s, Cardin learnt through experience the importance of balancing profits against the prestige of the designer name.

canned fish and fruit and baby-buggies meant that Cardin suffered the subsequent loss of prestige customers who had previously associated the Cardin name with the best in French design. Still smarting from the experience, Cardin has reorganized his licensing procedures and it is hoped that the 'name' will regain some of its lost prestige.

DEVELOPMENTS IN RETAILING
Mail order

Not all fashion merchandise is destined for retailers, whether they are franchises, department stores, speciality stores, chain stores, multiples or independently owned boutiques. During the 1980s, mail-order catalogues underwent something of a transformation. Once considered downmarket, in Britain catalogues were given a facelift by George Davis when he launched the *Next Directory*, which not only offered fashionable and quality garments but was itself beautifully designed and presented. Existing catalogue companies took notice of the huge market interest and began to enlist the help of named designers, well-known fashion models and photographers: the 'upmarket' catalogue company Kingsmill now retails designs by Paul Costello, Margaret Howell and Caroline Charles.

In the USA, where many of the well-known department stores had historic links with catalogues, the 1980s saw a reverse trend, with many catalogue famous names like Montgomery Ward and Sears, Roebuck and Company discontinuing their catalogue business as they concentrated on retail store activities. Nevertheless, some new catalogue companies did emerge: J. Crew and L.L. Bean now compete alongside Lands End, Bachrach, Talbot's and giants in the field Spiegel.

Related to catalogues are the 'magalogues', another venture launched by George Davis via the British tabloid newspaper the *Daily Express*. The idea behind the magalogue was that it would be sold on a monthly basis like a magazine but customers could direct-order what they saw for 'next-day' delivery. Unlike traditional catalogues, Davis's magalogue did not offer credit terms (the possibility for customers to pay for garments in weekly or monthly instalments), but the idea was developed and was relaunched as *Xtend* and encouraged the

appearance of other magalogues by companies like Racing Green.

Electronic shopping

A developing area of non-store-based retailing is 'home shopping' via the television and telephone from Cable Value Network, the Home Shopping Network and QVC. Home shopping continues to grow in popularity, although it may be some time yet before the European designer ready-to-wear collections are available to us by this means! Some companies are also experimenting with video catalogues: for some time videos of *couture* collections have been available to private customers who are unable to attend the openings.

Some stores are also testing video order machines (similar to the automated banking machines) outside their stores. Even when the store is closed, customers can still view a video of merchandise on offer and, using a charge card, order the things they see and have them delivered to their home.

With the increasing availability of home computers, it will not be long before manufacturers will have to reconsider their marketing policies to include Web sites in order to reach the potentially huge international market. Interactive, multimedia fashion shows on the Internet may not be that far off!

BRANDS AND BRANDING

An aspect of marketing that is often misunderstood and frequently overlooked is branding. Branding is not just about having a prominent name, it is a powerful marketing concept and the result of a carefully orchestrated range of activities across the whole spectrum of the marketing mix of the 'Four Ps': product, price, promotion and place.

The purpose of branding is to help achieve and maintain a loyal customer base in a cost-effective way in order to achieve the highest possible returns on an investment. While branding has been used ever since mankind had something to exchange in the marketplace – either goods or services – as a marketing concept, it has developed most in the past hundred years or so as a result of the increased and more complex nature of manufacturing processes and distribution networks, changes in retailing systems and increasingly sophisticated consumers. The 1990s have been called the 'decade of the brand', since this marketing concept is now of central importance to a wide range of companies in a wide range of industries operating in the global marketplace.

ORIGINS

The word 'brand' is derived from the Old Norse word *brandr*, meaning 'to burn', and burning brands were and continue to be the means by which livestock owners identify and differentiate their animals from those owned by others. From the branding of livestock, it was a short step to the branding of wares.

In Greek and Roman times, shopkeepers hung signs outside their stores to indicate the type of goods or services they offered, and manufacturers such as potters would brand or place their identifying mark – perhaps a thumb-print or an incised pattern in the still-wet clay – to identify their own products. The potter hoped that customers would look for his mark or brand when they were buying, and customers also benefited from the brands because they could avoid products that had proven unsatisfactory in the past. Early branding was thus both a sign of authorship and a way of differentiating products.

ADDED VALUES

Branded products are different to commodities. The commodities market is characterized by the fact that consumers do not differentiate between different manufacturers or suppliers – one pot is

Louis Vuitton luggage and accessories are sold only in exclusive Louis Vuitton shops:
Bangkok, G1 Peninsula Plaza, Tel. 2549083 • The Oriental Hotel, Tel. 2360420 ext. 3372.

LOUIS VUITTON

Brand power: not just a handbag, but a Louis Vuitton handbag that comes ready loaded with those 'added values'.

very much like another pot. With commodity goods, in many cases our decision to purchase is often made on the basis of price or availability, not on the basis of the brand or manufacturer's name. The difference between a commodity and a brand is what is often described as 'added values'. A brand product embodies additional attributes which some may consider intangible but are nevertheless very real to the consumer.

In fashion – in areas like clothing, cosmetics, personal care products like shampoos and with perfumes – the added values are often simply emotional, and the brands are therefore symbolic devices. In fashion, brands are bought and used primarily because they help consumers 'express something about themselves' to their peer groups. It is not necessarily the functional

capabilities of the product that are important to us: a woman does not buy a bottle of branded or 'famous-name' perfume simply because she wants to smell nice, or a brand name handbag because she needs a container in which to put all her 'bits and bobs'. She buys a brand because it communicates something about herself through its design, packaging, her recollections of the advertising, the notions of the quality of the contents or manufacturing process, the price she has paid and the effort she made in seeking out and selecting the retailer who stocks that brand of perfume or handbag.

The marketing mix of product, price, promotion and place attempts to persuade consumers that the added values are in some ways unique to a particular perfume or handbag

61

N°5

Chanel No 5: that sweet smell of success. It is a brand leader in its market, commanding considerable customer loyalty.

international branding consultancy Interbrand, of the world's top 50 brands, seven are from the world of fashion and fashion-related products: Chanel No.5, Levis, Estée Lauder, Marks & Spencer, Gillette, Rolex and Dunhill. In Interbrand's evaluation, these brands are strong for a number of reasons. First, they are brand leaders in their market sector and are consequently a more stable, powerful and profitable property than others in their sector. Second, they are long-established brands which command consumer loyalty and have therefore become an integral part of the fabric of the fashion market.

MARKET LEADERS
Levis

In 1850, a young entrepreneur called Levi Strauss selected denim (from *serge de Nîmes*, a type of heavy cotton cloth which originated in Nîmes in France) as the fabric for hard-wearing work trousers for the miners working in the Californian gold fields. Strauss also chose the indigo dye and in 1873 added the patented copper rivets to the pockets of the trousers because miners had complained that the weight of their tools caused them to rip. Levi jeans are largely unchanged from the time they were first introduced, but the company is now the world's largest clothing manufacturer.

As a brand, Levi jeans have a number of unique features: they were the first denim jeans and therefore have an unmatched pedigree; furthermore, they have certain proprietary design features, including the orange double arch of

and that other perfumes or handbags cannot emulate them, or find difficult it to do so. Because consumers recognize and appreciate the added values of successful brands, manufacturers and retailers are able to charge significantly higher prices for brands compared to equivalent commodities – 'ordinary' perfumes or handbags.

The aim of transforming a fashion product from a mere commodity into a powerful, long-lasting brand is something of a paradox given that it is the nature of fashion to be 'for the moment' and constantly changing. Nevertheless, in the fashion industry a number of major brands have succeeded in this task and have established fashions which transcend short-term shifts in consumer taste. According to the

Levi jeans may have remained largely unchanged since they were first introduced but the company itself is now the world's largest clothing manufacturer.

stitching on the back pockets and the orange copper rivets. Wrangler, the world's number 2 jeans company and a major brand of the giant VF Corporation, claim to have given the world the first denim jeans designed to fit the body rather than hang off it, yet Levis continue to be the number 1 jeans by developing and sustaining the brand's added values in tune with changing market needs.

During the 1980s, at the height of the 'designer denims' wars, Levi Strauss was unable to gain a foothold in this valuable market. As consumers' attitudes to denims changed, Levis went back to producing what the company had originally made – Levi 501s. While retaining the core values of the jeans – 'Americanness', toughness and masculinity – Levis coupled them with nostalgic images which appealed to the youth market: 1950s retro in the form of Nick Kamen in a fifties-style launderette doing his washing to the sound of Marvin Gaye's 'I Heard it Through the Grapevine' proved a winner. The advert was not selling jeans, but sex appeal and the notion of a 'design classic'.

Levi Strauss are not the only fashion brand to have been around for the last hundred years or so: Aquascutum, Hermès and Louis Vuitton are all long-established brands and leaders in their market sectors.

Model No. G.9

Model No. G.10

The Famous "Aquascutum" Storm Coats

THE centre illustration above (No. G.9) depicts our world famous Storm coat. This was originally designed for the rigorous conditions created by trench warfare, and is one of the most successful weatherproof coats yet designed. It is, however, equally suitable for either civil or military conditions where absolute security against torrential rain is desired. It is made of the finest quality Egyptian cotton, lined with self material and a special waterproof interlining, it has raglan sleeves, deep storm collar, large throat tab, strap cuffs, large D.B. lapels, a yoke back, and inside leg straps for riding. The shoulder straps are detachable. Ready-to-wear or made to measure.

Aquascutum Ltd.   *100 Regent St., London, W.1.*

Aquascutum advertising from earlier this century reflects the company's origins in 1851 as producers of waterproof wool coats.

Aquascutum

Aquascutum have been 'makers of fine clothes since 1851' and the original business was built on a process devised for showerproofing wool coats (the name Aquascutum is derived from the Latin for 'water shield'). The Aquascutum raincoat found its way onto the battlefield in Russia in 1855, and by the First World War had evolved into the 'trench coat'.

Now a luxury fashion brand for both men and women, the products sold under the Aquascutum label include classic raincoats as well as suits and accessories. Aquascutum brand products are now sold in over fifty countries, and more than half the company's profits are derived from non-UK sales: In Japan, Aquascutum is now one the most successful imported brands.

Hermès

Founded in 1837 by Emile Hermès, 90 per cent of the Hermès business, a luxury fashion goods manufacturer with an international reputation, remains in the hands of the founder's direct descendants.

Unlike other fashion companies such as Cardin or Dior, Hermès absolutely refuses to license the brand to third parties. Consequently, the majority of products bearing the Hermès brand name are made by the company in its own ateliers and workshops. And unlike many other fashion companies, Hermès is conservative in the use of its name, initials and logos on all its products.

Marks & Spencer

The British-based retailer Marks & Spencer can trace its origins back to 1882. Currently, it is estimated that the company has close to a 20 per cent share of all UK clothing sales and a 5 per cent share of UK food sales. The flagship Marble Arch store on London's Oxford Street is reckoned to have the fastest-moving stock in the world per square foot of retail space! As well as branches in Europe and North America, Marks & Spencer also owns Brooks Brothers, one of America's most well-known men's clothiers.

A peculiar policy of Marks & Spencer is its use of dual brands: the corporate brand is Marks & Spencer, yet even though the company does not sell any other manufacturer's brands in any of its stores, only its own-label goods, it uses a separate product brand name on its goods, St. Michael. The reasons for these dual brands are largely historical. In 1928, the St. Michael brand was introduced to allow Marks & Spencer's own products to have the same 'free-standing' status as other manufacturer's brands which at that time were also stocked by the company's stores and predominated in their sales. Over the years, other manufacturers' brands were eliminated until only St. Michael brand products were sold. Not sold in any other retail outlets, the St. Michael brand is the exclusive brand of Marks & Spencer.

Benetton and Swatch

New brands are extremely expensive to develop and launch, and furthermore it is a risky venture: an estimated 17 out of every 20 brands launched are failures. Nevertheless, in the fashion world new brands *have* succeeded, and notable successes are Benetton and Swatch. In less than twenty years, Benetton has established a powerful international brand reputation in a difficult and ever changing market sector.

In the early 1980s, the lower price sector of the Swiss watch industry was nearly destroyed by competition from the Japanese, who appeared to have overtaken the Swiss in terms of technology, production and marketing. In 1983, Swatch, an inexpensive quartz watch with half the moving parts of other quartz watches, was launched. By 1984, more than 3.5 million Swatch watches had been sold. The brand name, the low cost of the product and its design and fun advertising have all contributed to its success and have largely restored confidence in the Swiss mass-market watchmaking industry.

The next step for the Swatch brand is the launch of the 'Swatch Car'. Still largely at the concept stage, the car – from a country with no tradition of car manufacturing – is as fun and attractive (and no doubt will be as reliable) as the Swatch watch.

While Swatch and Benetton are relatively new brands, some brands that appear to be new are in fact much older, often because they have 'moved' from being a national brand well known in its country of origin to being an international brand and famous the world over. This shift to international prominence may take some time and careful planning.

Hugo Boss

Hugo Boss, the men's designer and clothes manufacturer, was founded in Germany in 1923 but it wasn't until 1972 that the company found its first export markets in Austria and Switzerland, with the Benelux countries, Scandinavia and the UK following shortly.

In 1977 the USA was added to Boss's export markets, but it was really when the company was selected to costume the male stars in popular US television shows like *Miami Vice*, *L.A. Law* and *Dynasty* that the Hugo Boss brand's international reputation was confirmed.

Reebok and Nike

Reebok can trace its origins back to Bolton in Lancashire in the 1880s, when the original Reebok running shoe was made. Only in 1979, when the US rights were sold to Paul Fireman, did the brand really begin to take off: Even in the UK, Reebok was still largely unknown in a market dominated by Adidas (named after its founder, Adi Dassler, who was making sports shoes in Herzogenarach in Germany as early as the 1920s).

In the 1980s, when aerobics became popular, careful marketing strategies encouraged public recognition of Reebok to the extent that it became the shoe for fitness fanatics. Celebrity endorsement in the shape of aerobics guru Jane Fonda encouraged sales, and by 1988 Reebok had high-impact sales in the USA of £1 billion (c. $1.8 billion).

With training shoes now a fashion item, for most consumers technical design and function are not the first concern: it is the brand name that we seek out from among the range of running shoes available. With Nike at the number 1 spot in branded sports shoes and Reebok at number 2, it is these labels that are most sought after, and their logos are valuable items that act as a sort of shorthand to recognizing the brand's added values.

Not surprisingly, these brands and their logos find themselves alongside other brands like Chanel, Hermès, Gucci, Rolex, Lacoste, Ralph Lauren's Polo and Louis Vuitton as victims of the counterfeit pirates producing 'knock-offs' (copies) of products bearing well-known brand names and logos – the identifying devices that consumers have depended on as guarantees of

[Top] Reebok 'Shaq™nosis'. Although the company has been around since the 1880s, it wasn't until 1979 that the Reebok brand gained international recognition.

The famous crocodile logo on a Lacoste sports shirt [left] and the distinctive VL initial design on Louis Vuitton leather goods [above] are the devices that consumers have long relied on as guarantees of quality and authenticity – and as carriers of 'added values' such as exclusivity. Increasingly, however, brand names and logos have fallen prey to the counterfeit pirates.

manufacture and quality but also as carriers of added values. In the mid-1980s it was estimated that over 90 per cent of so-called 'Louis Vuitton' luggage sold in the world was counterfeit!

MARKET SHARE

The added values that are inherent in fashion brands have thus proven to be lucrative assets to be exploited. With less than 10 per cent of designers' revenues coming from *haute couture*, most of the leading European designers and houses have found that the bulk of their company's income is derived from brand licensing activities in areas such as perfumes and cosmetics. According to the US Department of Commerce, in 1990 Americans were spending more than £11.5 billion ($18.5 billion) a year on fragrances, cosmetics and toiletries – and that does not include soaps! Yves Saint Laurent brands include Opium (the company's best selling brand), Paris, Rive Gauche, Kouros and Jazz; Chanel brands include brand leader in perfumes Chanel No.5, Coco, Chanel No.19 and men's fragrance Anteus. Meanwhile, Dior's leading brands include Miss Dior, Diorella and Diorissimo.

According to *Business Week* (31 July 1985), Estée Lauder, with its four leading brands of Estée Lauder, Clinique, Aramis and Prescriptives, is the leading manufacturer of prestige cosmetics and fragrances and commands around 50 per cent of the total market share. Boasting around 13 per cent of the market, second-placed Cosmair's brands include L'Oreal, Lancôme, Biotherm and designer fragrances. Wander

around any department store perfume section and take a look at the manufacturers' names on those famous brands! Third place in the market is held by the giant Unilever, which manufactures the brands of Timotei (the best selling shampoo in the world outside the USA), Calvin Klein, Fabergé and Elizabeth Arden (the Elizabeth Arden line also includes the 'Elizabeth Taylor' fragrances Passion, White Diamonds and the Fragrant Jewels Collection).

Avon started life in the 1880s as the California Perfume Company and specialized in good-quality yet inexpensive perfumes sold through canvassing agents. Its first product was the Little Dot Perfume Set, a collection of five different scents. By 1928, the name California Perfume Company was seen as too restrictive for a business successfully trading across the USA, and following a visit to England by the company's founder David McConnell – who decided that the land around the Suffern laboratory looked a little like the countryside of Shakespeare's birthplace, Stratford-upon-Avon – the official corporate title was changed to Avon Products Inc. With annual sales of over £1.8 billion ($3 billion), Avon is one of the largest and best-known brands of fragrances, cosmetics and personal care products. Avon Products' annual income is augmented by revenue derived from its other brands, including Giorgio and Oscar de la Renta.

Recent expansion by Proctor and Gamble, creators of the disposable diaper in the 1960s, and the largest producer of detergents and soaps, has led the company into the market of

VIDAL SASSOON

Crowning glory: Vidal Sassoon's 'own label' range of hair care products was sold to Proctor and Gamble who had also acquired famous names like Head and Shoulders, Max Factor, Mary Quant and Covergirl.

personal-care products. Already owning successful brands of hair-care products like Head and Shoulders, Proctor and Gamble acquired two major divisions from Revlon: Max Factor (with a 5 per cent share of the mass market) and Betrix (a brand popular in Germany, Eastern Europe and the leading brand in Japan) as well as the Mary Quant line and the fragrances California and Le Jardin. In addition, the products of the Noxell Corporation – Covergirl (with a huge 23 per cent of the US mass market and growing in Europe), Clarion and Noxzema have been merged into Proctor and Gamble.

Credit must also go to Proctor and Gamble for realizing the brand potential of the Vidal Sassoon range of hair-care products. Originally an 'own-label' brand sold through Sassoon's salons, the brand was sold to Proctor and Gamble, who developed it into the successful international brand with a reputation for excellence.

THE IMPORTANCE OF BRANDING

Manufacturers invest a great deal of time and money in branding for a number of reasons. If a trademark has been registered, the manufacturer has a legally protected right to an exclusive brand name which allows it to develop and establish a unique identity for the product which it can reinforce through its marketing activities like advertising. This in turn increases opportunities to attract large numbers of consumers and encourage them to make repeat purchases of the product, and helps to establish brand recognition among potential new customers.

With the high costs and the risks involved in developing new brands, however, the emphasis in recent years has been on existing brand development and line extensions. Designers like Giorgio Armani, Donna Karan and Calvin Klein have increased the number of their lines to include 'bridge collections' – lower-priced clothing that carries the added values perceived in the brand name but at a lower retail price. Manufacturers with a pedigree of strong brands are more likely to find distributors more receptive to these brand extensions, and retailers also see these strong brands as important since the manufacturer's activities – such as advertising – result in faster turnover of stock. Some retailers are also interested in stocking only well-known brands since they believe that the positive image of the brand and its added values enhance their own shop image.

Meanwhile, if we remember that as consumers we use brand names as a method of identifying products in the marketplace, brands make shopping a less time-consuming activity, and in the world of fashion goods, brands satisfy those 'intangible needs' for things like enhanced status through their added values.

Pop star and actor Marky Mark shows his Calvin Klein underpants on the catwalk.

PLANNING AHEAD

Since the word 'fashion' implies a continuous state of change, everyone involved in the fashion industry – textile producers, garment manufacturers and retailers – needs to be able to absorb an enormous quantity of information in order to anticipate change and predict consumer preferences.

FORECASTING

Because retailers need to buy fashions that their customers will want to wear and because the garment manufacturers have to work so far in advance of the selling season, both retailers and manufacturers must also be fashion forecasters. Fashion forecasting involves the evaluation of the designer's collections. Traditionally, manufacturers and retailers turn to Paris and Milan for suggestions for new trends, but increasingly, both are looking at other fashion centres, especially the USA, the UK and Japan.

Designs

At first glance, it may seem as though most of the designers are 'doing the same thing' and that there is little difference between them. However, close evaluation of each collection can reveal the subtle differences between each designer's work even though they may be using similar themes drawn from contemporary culture or contemporary events.

When a number of designers use a common theme, it may be an indication of a new fashion trend. A designer's whole idea or entire collection may not become a trend – it may be that only a particular fabrication, the overall silhouette or even a single garment or accessory serves as the 'statement' of a trend.

Market segments

A second aspect of fashion forecasting is evaluating which segment of the market will accept a particular fashion. Today, diverse consumer lifestyles have helped to create many separate niche markets, and each have their own fashion trends, although sometimes a popular trend may spread to all areas of the market.

While the designer fashions seen on the catwalks of Paris, Milan and London are often 'extreme' fashions, retailers must decide which 'looks' will suit their customers. For affluent customers or those with a high public profile such as movie or rock stars, often only the original 'catwalk collection look' will do. Other customers in different age groups and with

The look created for the catwalk by Donna Karan will eventually become edited for retail consumption. While the main garments and the overall silhouette may be retained, details such as the ankle socks and hats may disappear once the line is released.

different lifestyles and disposable incomes favour other 'looks', and because it is some time between the first appearance of the original fashion idea and when the mass-market customers adopt it, an important aspect of fashion forecasting is researching into the timing of fashion trend adoption.

KEEPING UP WITH TRENDS

Without travelling to the world's fashion centres, fashion designers (who are not usually invited to shows anyway!) and store buyers are able to learn about new fashion trends from a number of design-reporting services. Known variously as 'fashion consultants', 'fashion reporting services' or 'fashion predictors', their main service is to provide immediate, accurate and in-depth information about designers' collections.

Generally, the reporting services attend both the *couture* and *prêt-à-porter* shows, where they photograph the collections and make sketches and notes about individual 'statement' garments, silhouettes and details of fastenings and trims. They then prepare written reports which are mailed to their subscribers about a week after the collections are shown. In addition, most fashion forecasting consultancies offer their own guides to the coming season which include fabric swatches, colour samples and design interpretations. Individual fashion companies often employ forecasters to give slide and video presentations of their predictions for the next season.

Accurate forecasting of colour trends is vital not only for textile producers, fashion designers and garment manufacturers. The giant cosmetics industry will also use this information to develop ranges to complement the coming season's colours.trends.

The services provided by forecasters are not inexpensive, but most subscribers have found that the cost is warranted by the speed and accuracy of the information that forecasters provide. As a specialized service to the fashion industry, many forecasting consultancies were born in the 1960s alongside the rise in numbers of new young designers and the advent of designer *prêt-à-porter*, but some prediction services have been around for much longer.

Tobé Associates

One of the oldest and most prestigious of the fashion prediction consultancies is Tobé Associates, founded in 1927 by Tobé Coller Davis. With a unique skill for analysing fashions and predicting trends, Tobé began publishing the highly successful weekly *Tobé Report*. Although she died in 1962, the *Tobé Report* continues and a staff of fashion writers and editors cover the major fashion markets in Europe and the USA. Alongside their interpretations and evaluations of the collections, Tobé Associates provide detailed data on prices and manufacturers. In addition to the written reports, video presentations of fashion forecasts called *Tobé on Tape* are also available.

Accurate information in a fast-changing industry is a valuable commodity, and fees for the services of Tobé Associates are based on the dollar-volume of the stores of their subscribers: the bigger the store turnover, the more expensive the reports.

Other services

Other major reporting and forecasting consultancies are the New York City-based IM International, which produces *The Action Report* covering the New York ready-to-wear and Paris/Milan collections. London-based Nigel French reports on European and American fashions and knitwear which are of particular interest to textile mills and manufacturers, but French also specializes in coverage of the Mode-Woche and the Paris 'pret' collections, as well as being a leader in forecasting significant trends in home furnishings. 'Lifestyle' design is a lucrative area into which many fashion designers have recently ventured: Ralph Lauren, Calvin Klein, Mulberry, Laura Ashley, Joseph, Yves Saint Laurent and Pierre Cardin are just a few who now have lines of designer bed linens and furnishing fabrics. The Fashion Service presents twelve monthly reporting folios for its clients as well as *Fashion Forecast*, a quarterly report on trends in colour and fabric for the major seasons, and *Info-Flash*, a monthly menswear report.

Promostyl, a leading international design and fashion forecasting office with its headquarters in Paris, also designs over 200 collections each year for major textile manufacturers and apparel manufacturers as well as designing 'private labels' for retail by department stores. Large retail store groups now compete with manufacturers by creating their own brands, commissioning designs to be made by manufacturers or special merchandise to be produced by contractors that will be exclusive to their chain of stores. The store buyer may select a garment that he or she predicts will be *the* popular item of the next selling season and have it copied in the Far East, India or Turkey. The store can then put its own label on the merchandise or perhaps gives it label bearing the name of a fictitious designer. While private labels do encourage customer loyalty because the merchandise is not available in any other store, it has proven to be most successful in menswear, which is traditionally brand-based and concentrates on basic items of clothing. Private-label women's fashion garments frequently end up on the sale racks at the end of the season, however.

Video has proven to be a useful medium for fashion forecasting reports: as customers, we are now well used to seeing in-store video presentations of designer collections. For the retail store buyer, Videofashion Inc. offers *Videofashion News* (12 videos a year showing the major designer collections and themes), *Videofashion Monthly* (12 issues which also feature comment and interviews with major designers) as well as *Videofashion Specials* and *Videofashion Men*. In addition, there are newsletters and industry surveys that help the store buyers and designers forecast and source ideas.

Fashion Calendar lists the dates and venues of collection openings and major market weeks, while trade publications offer information not only on fashion trends but developments in the fashion industry as a whole. The major fashion newspaper is *Womens Wear Daily*. Published five times a week, each day it focuses on different topics. The bi-monthly condensed version is *W*, which is published in colour. In France, the major trade magazine is *Gap*, while England has *Draper's Record* and *Fashion Weekly*. For menswear, Fairchild Publications, the leading voice in fashion matters, produces *Daily News Record*, while four times a year *Gentlemen's Quarterly* provides trend reports covering the Milan and Paris menswear shows. Around five thousand copies of the report are sent to retailers to help keep them abreast of new ideas in the market. Meanwhile, the children's fashion market is covered by *Earnshaws*, *Kids Fashions* and *Children's Business*, and sportswear is handled by the leading trade magazine *Sportswear International*.

BUYERS

The essential link in the fashion marketing chain is the store buyer. For fashion to move from the catwalk and manufacturers' showroom into the retail store, a buyer has to purchase it.

The buyer's job, which is often seen as one of the most glamorous in the fashion industry, is to predict and buy in enough quantity, in enough sizes and colours, at the right price, the garments they believe will be the next selling season's 'ford' (a popular style). Often the buyer will negotiate a special or exclusive deal with a designer or manufacturer for their stores: 'exclusive to' merchandise to retailers like Browns on South Molton Street, Harvey Nichols at Knightsbridge or Barney's in New York not only gives the stores credibility and prestige but provides security and equivalent prestige for

Actress Demi Moore at the Versace show. The marketing potential of movie stars is such that many designers lend entire *prêt-à-porter* wardrobes in exchange for endorsement.

those designers and manufacturers whose garments are stocked only at top-name stores.

Consequently, designers and manufacturers 'look after' store buyers as well as they look after the fashion press who report on their collections. At the major shows, the best seats are reserved for the fashion editors of the major glossy magazines and the 'trades' – John Fairchild is guaranteed one of the best seats in the house – the retail buyers of the 'important stores' and celebrity customers whose presence serves as product endorsement.

Types of buying office

The buyer's job also involves the more mundane though equally important role of getting their store's customers to buy the merchandise they have selected. When not abroad on buying trips, Joan Burstein, the owner-buyer for Browns, and her team will be found on the shop floor with their customers. Browns run what is known as a *private resident* buying office, which serves the company exclusively.

The cost of maintaining such a buying office can be high, and generally it is only the top speciality stores like Browns and Harvey Nichols or giant chains and department stores that can afford to do so. In the USA, Montgomery Ward have private resident offices in New York, Los Angeles, Dallas, Miami and Chicago to help them turn over the huge volume of sales from their 500 or so stores and mail-order businesses. Nieman Marcus staffs a *private resident buying office* in New York in order to maintain the Texas store's leading image as one of the top American high-fashion and high-quality retailers.

A private resident buying office is just one type of buying office. A resident buying office may serve as an adviser and buying representative for one or more non-competing, related stores. Stores are considered non-competitive when they are situated a 'suitable' distance away from each other, perhaps in a different city – and therefore don't compete for the same customers.

Resident buying offices do not replace the store's own buyers, nor are they 'open to buy' – they do not have a budget that can be spent on merchandise to be delivered within a given period minus the amount allocated to goods on order. Instead, resident buyers assist store buyers in an advisory capacity. The majority of resident buying offices are independent businesses which charge their members (their client-stores they service) a fee which is generally based on each store's volume sales and the amount and type of services used by the store. Some of these *independent buying offices* are small: they may consist of only be one highly experienced buyer servicing a select number of non-competing stores, such as London-based independent buyer Sarah Le Marquand. Other independent resident buying offices like the Donegar Group operate 11 divisions and represent over 500 stores. Some independents specialize in high-quality fashions from the leading designers, while others specialize in the lower end of the fashion market, assisting stores which sell less expensive apparel. Others may offer expertise in specific market areas such as leather goods, furs, jewellery and accessories.

A third type of buying office is the *corporate resident buying office*. This is owned and maintained by a parent company or its stores. Often the parent company has built a chain of retail stores by acquiring or merging with formerly independent retailers. Examples are R.H. May and Company and Sears Roebuck. Because the formerly independent stores may differ from each other – they may even retain the trading name familiar to customers prior to the take-over or merger – the corporate buying office often finds itself servicing a variety of often dissimilar stores in different countries: for

example, Sears not only has stores in the USA but also has major retail stores like Selfridges on London's Oxford Street.

The fourth type, *co-operative resident buying offices* (also referred to as 'associated offices'), are owned and maintained by a group of non-competing, non-related (independent of each other in terms of ownership) and privately owned stores which jointly support the work of the co-operative buying office through fees which depend on the services used and each store's volume sales. Co-operative buying offices often limit 'members' or clients to stores with similar merchandise policies, sales volumes or types of customers, and new 'members' often have to wait to be invited to join the service. One of the best-known co-operative buying offices is the Associated Merchandising Corporation. AMC was founded in 1918 in New York and today represents clients like F. & R. Lazarus of Cincinnati, J.L. Hudson of Detroit and Foleys of Houston. Until recently, AMC also serviced Federated Department Stores (including Bloomingdales, Abraham and Straus and Filenes) until Federated opened its own corporate office. One of the major services offered by AMC is assistance with imported goods, and in addition to its US offices, AMC has offices in London, Paris, the Far East, Australia and South America. The international division of AMC services such retail stores as Saks Fifth Avenue (part of Investcorps) and Sears.

Bloomingdales, whose buying office is maintained by its parent corporation, Federated Department Stores.

SOURCES

Buyers will purchase new fashions from new sources and from 'key sources' – manufacturers who have maintained a reputation for reliability, quality fabrication and whose merchandise sells well because of its styling and/or price. Buying from these manufacturers' lines is known as 'line buying', but buyers are also always on the lookout for merchandise which is new and innovative, known as 'trend buying'.

In order to have a full range of garments for sale the next season, buyers have to visit the showrooms of many manufacturers. This is because most garment manufacturers generally specialize in manufacture according to either size, type of garment or price range. In terms of size specialization, a buyers' job is made more difficult because there is no national – let alone international – standardization of sizes!

Manufacturers also specialize in producing *types* of apparel: dresses (either one or two pieces – a dress with a jacket perhaps), sportswear (co-ordinated separates like blouses, jackets, pants or active sportswear), swim and beachwear, maternity wear, intimate apparel, outerwear (coats, suits and rainwear), evening wear, bridal wear and uniforms for workers in catering, healthcare, airlines, etc.

CO-ORDINATION

One of the main concerns of the retail store fashion buyer is to ensure that all the pieces of an outfit – the jacket, blouse or sweater, skirt or trousers and overcoat – that they saw modelled on the catwalk or in the designer's showroom

The Armani store: ultimate success in the fashion industry is achieved at retail level where consumer acceptance is measured in purchases.

and which are all made by different manufacturers in different parts of the world arrive in the store's stock receiving area in the right colours, the right sizes and in the right numbers at the right price and at the right time, ready to go out onto the sales floor at the start of the season!

Purchase orders written by buyers specify the date of order, the terms of sale (how soon and by what method or currency the invoice will be paid, and any discount negotiated), shipping instructions (land, sea or air freight), the shipping address (since the stock receiving area may not be located inside the store but off-site), quantity (some items are bought individually, others are bought in dozens – ties are sold in dozens, and buyers have to remember to order not 12 of a style but 1 of a style, otherwise they would find themselves having to pay for and sell not a dozen but 144 ties!), colour and price.

When merchandise arrives at a retailer's store room, any differences between the original order and the actual shipment must be reconciled and a decision made to accept or reject partly filled orders or any errors or substitutions made by the manufacturers. Some retailers use 'charge backs' to withhold payments to their sources to compensate for manufacturers' mistakes or an incorrect assortment. Once the garments are in the retailers' premises they must be insured against loss, theft and damage. Stocktaking is not just about counting how many pieces of stock are in the shop (which should tally against the number originally bought and the receipts showing how many have been sold) but assessing the cost of insuring the remaining stock.

Once on the shop floor, the retail buyer becomes a seller. Whatever the level of the fashion industry, the aim is the same: to sell.

The traditional quality and craftsmanship of bespoke tailoring at Henry Poole and Co. is emphasized by the furnishing of their showrooms.

PUBLIC RELATIONS

It is often thought that public relations is a relatively new development, but PR has been around for a long time. Defined by the Institute of Public Relations as 'a deliberate, planned and sustained effort to establish and maintain goodwill and mutual understanding between an organisation and its publics', PR is not simply about creating a favourable image, smartening up a tarnished one or creating a favourable climate of opinion; it is about creating understanding through knowledge, which often involves effecting change. PR is a form of communication which applies to any sort of organization – small or large, commercial or non-commercial, public or private sector. Consequently, PR can be said to have been in existence since the earliest civilizations, ever since one culture or group of people had something to say to another, whether in war or in peace!

One of the oldest forms of 'created' public relations is the house journal. Charles Dickens, in his book *American Notes* published in 1842 records the *Lowell Offering*, a house journal which was edited by the women who were working in a New England cotton mill. When

I.M. Singer began selling his sewing machines in America in 1855, he published his *Gazette* to give his customers information on how to use his machines. Around the same time, the Lever Brothers, who owned the Sunlight Soap factory in Liverpool and had built their workers the model 'garden city' of Port Sunlight, also published an employee journal. In Singer's case, the public at which his house journal was aimed was commercial. With the Lever Brothers, the target was their employees.

In initiatives for effecting social change, public relations techniques have also been used by governments: In Britain in 1809, the Treasury appointed a press spokesman, and in 1854 the Post Office published its first annual report in which it realized the importance of explaining to the British public exactly what it did and what services it offered to them. In 1912, when Lloyd George was Chancellor of the Exchequer, he organized a team of lecturers to explain the government's new 'old age pension scheme'. One of the most concerted PR efforts by the British

One of the names synonymous with fashion PR, Lynne Franks.

government was that organized by Sir Stephen Tallents between 1926 and 1933 on behalf of the Empire Marketing Board. £1 million (c. $1.6 million) was spent on posters, films and exhibitions to make the products of the British Empire better known in Britain. Tallents became the first president of the Institute of Public Relations in 1948, and today the industry's award takes the form of the Tallents Medal.

The Public Relations Society of America was also formed in 1948, but one of the first PR consultancies in the USA was set up by a journalist called Ivy Ledbetter Lee who handled PR first for the anthracite coal industry, then the Pennsylvania Railroad, and in 1914 became the PR adviser to oil tycoon John D. Rockefeller. Lee's job could not have been an easy one since he had to inform the press and public fairly and accurately about mining and railway disasters and industrial disputes. Lee's success at PR was largely due to his ability to create better relations between his clients and the press, and he established basic principles for press relations. In 1906, in a statement to the press, Lee promised that he would always supply prompt and accurate information concerning subjects about which it was in the public's interest to know.

DEFINING PR

Following the World Assembly of Public Relations Associations held in Mexico in 1978, the following statement was agreed: 'Public relations practice is the art and social science of analysing trends, predicting their consequences, counselling organisation leaders and implementing planned programmes of action which will serve both the organisation's and the public's interests.' Like Lee's statement, one of the main aspects of this definition of PR is its responsibility to the public's interest. An organization is judged on its behaviour, and PR is about goodwill and reputation.

Good PR is good business sense, since we all like to buy from and sell to and work for companies or organizations we know and trust. Because of this, most companies, whatever their size – from individual designer to giant multinational – undertake PR activities, either in-house or by engaging PR consultants, as part of their marketing activity.

Public relations in the fashion industry is often regarded as one of the most high-profile and glamorous of all marketing activities. Indeed, some of the best-known names in fashion PR – Lynne Franks, Janine du Plessis, Jean Bennet and Stephanie Churchill in the UK, and Eleanor Lambert (the creator of the Coty Fashion Awards), Ruth Hammer and Rosemary Sheehan in the USA – are as well known as some of the clients they represent. Nevertheless, much of the hard work of fashion PR consultants goes largely unnoticed by the general public: we are often only aware of their presence at major fashion events such as catwalk shows. Yet a fashion PR's work must be continuous, carefully organised throughout the fashion year, and they must have an in-depth knowledge of the entire fashion market from manufacturer to wholesaler and retailer.

What PR is not

Although it is closely involved with marketing, advertising and promotion, public relations can nevertheless be distinguished from these areas.

While marketing is defined by the CIM (Chartered Institute of Marketing) as 'the management process responsible for identifying, anticipating and satisfying customer requirements', the main concern of PR is effective communication aimed at groups of people other than just a company's customers.

The IPA (Institute of Practitioners in Advertising) defines advertising as the most persuasive possible selling message for a product or service, aimed at the right customers at the lowest possible cost. The emphasis in advertising is on selling, while the PR's role is to inform and create understanding through knowledge. If PR activity has created understanding and knowledge about a product or service, subsequent advertising will find it easier to sell it! PR is not a form of advertising, because PR relates to all the communications in an organization, whereas advertising is restricted largely to the marketing function. Furthermore, PR is not 'free advertising', because it is an activity planned throughout the year and time is money – either in the form of salaries for in-house PR staff or fees to PR consultants. Unlike advertising space in a magazine, newspaper or on television which can be accurately costed and budgeted, the communications generated by a PR that appear in editorial space in the mass media providing knowledge and information is priceless! While we may admire adverts for their artfulness, no matter how persuasive their message, we always remain that little bit sceptical. But if the same product or service is mentioned in editorial articles, it appears to have been 'tested', recommended or 'given the seal of approval' by people we believe in and trust for leadership.

Another form of communications with which PR is often confused is propaganda. Propaganda, which has an equally long history as PR, can best be described as a means of gaining support for an opinion or belief. Propaganda largely concentrates on emotional, intellectual or spiritual topics such as causes, politics or religion, with which some people may not agree. For the recipient of a propaganda message there is often no tangible gain: recipients may only 'feel' some inner satisfaction. Like advertising, propaganda is prejudiced in favour of its topic. Good PR, on the other hand, is factual and unbiased, and while propaganda and advertising are likely to invite suspicion or at least some disagreement, successful PR must be wholly credible.

PR must also be distinguished from publicity. Publicity is the result of information being made known. As we know, publicity can either be good or bad, but both are the result of the behaviour or activity of an individual or company, its products or services. The PR's role is to put right the causes of bad publicity, whether it is bad behaviour or bad information. Polishing a tarnished image is useless if what has created the tarnish in the first place is not dealt with!

PR IN FASHION

In the fashion industry today, fashion PR plays an increasingly important role which is reflected in the growth of the fashion PR industry itself over the past ten years or so. The 'bible' of fashion public relations, *Fashion Monitor*, now lists close to 200 PR companies with listed fashion accounts. Yet despite the increased amount of available expertise, many of the well-known fashion designers, including Giorgio Armani and Katharine Hamnett, as well as some large retailers like Marks & Spencer, continue to handle their PR activities in-house.

It is important to remember that the different parts of the fashion industry will have different PR needs because they are addressing different publics. For example, Soviet jeans were launched in Italy and France in presentations aimed directly at the trade staged in railway stations (to recreate the atmosphere of the Russian classics *Anna Karenina* and *Dr. Zhivago*!). The idea that the PR company was trying to put across was that Soviet jeans had arrived directly from Russia. In Continental Europe, where fashion distribution is mainly dominated by the smaller independent shops, promotion of Soviet jeans had to be aimed at the fashion industry as a whole. In the UK, however, the Soviet jeans launch was targeted directly at the retail consumer because a distribution network in the form of the large chain stores was already in place. In the UK, chain stores carry out a large proportion of PR activity, both for their own products and services as well as in conjunction with the designers whose lines they carry.

An industrial body such as the British Fashion Council (whose PR is handled by Life PR, formerly known as Lynne Franks PR) speaks to a wide audience of industrialists, legislators and financiers. Retailers, on the other hand, need to communicate more directly with the retail shopper, while designers need to communicate with the retail store buyers who actually buy the goods, and with the manufacturers who will produce them. Consequently, the work carried out by the fashion PR office – whether in-house or a specialist fashion PR agency – will vary depending on their client's needs and place in the industry. Nevertheless, in the course of the year, the PR's activities will generally involve press relations, organizing publicity material and resources, corporate communications and fashion events.

Cultivating the press

Developing and maintaining good relations with the press is one of the key activities of the fashion PR. This needs to be done throughout the year, not just when a new collection or new designer fragrance is about to be launched. In the fashion industry, press relations are important for two reasons: First, fashion products have a very short life cycle and have restricted seasons. Second, there is an enormous amount of competition between designers, manufacturers and retailers.

Journalists and editors on the trade newspapers, glossy fashion magazines and national newspapers need to be kept informed of industry developments. The trade press needs facts such as wholesale prices, fabrics, colour details and manufacturers' names. The consumer press, on the other hand, needs style details, retail prices and stockists' names and addresses. Although it is the newspapers and magazines which provide the fashion news for the consumer, much of that news is provided to the media by the fashion PR. Increasingly, editors rely on PRs for news stories, articles, photographs, interviews and ideas for features, and many journalists are invited by the PR office to attend press events.

Types of press event

There are three types of press event: the press conference, the press reception and the facility visit.

A *press conference* is a meeting of journalists who have been assembled, often at short notice, to receive information. The British Fashion Council used press conferences to gain media attention for their campaign to get more government backing for the British fashion industry. The important feature of press conferences is that communication is a two-way process: the press can ask questions of individuals – designers or company directors – who have to answer on the spot.

A *press reception* is a more organized formal event, often with catered hospitality (a bar, buffet or lunch) and a programme of talks, demonstrations and perhaps an audio-visual presentation. Often the PR will also arrange for special or exclusive interviews with the leading designers. With the pop-star status of many

designers today, competition for media coverage is fierce, and part of the PR specialist's job is to know which interviews are likely to be read, seen or heard by the key target markets for their client's designs. An interview with Jean-Paul Gaultier is more likely to be of interest to the readers of *Elle* and therefore more useful to the designer in terms of publicity than the same interview with a representative of *Woman's Own*! Likewise, the fashions worn by the Spice Girls are more likely to be of interest to teenage readers of magazines like *Jackie* and *Seventeen* than *Vogue*.

In a *facility visit*, journalists are taken to visit a manufacturer or to the new store or concession. The launch of the first Principles shop took place in the store, where invited journalists had the opportunity to view both the merchandise and the new store's interior layout before the public attended. As designers like Donna Karan, Christian Lacroix and Calvin Klein open flagship stores in the world's capital cities, press events like these are increasingly popular and successful methods of transmitting information to the fashion public.

THE PR'S JOB

Fashion PR doesn't just involve cultivating goodwill among those who can communicate to the mass of the public the latest developments in fashion and retailing, it is also about triggering action. Consequently, a PR's work can involve producing press releases and captioned photographs for which models will have been chosen and hired, and photographers, hair and

Press releases, receptions and photographs would prepare the media and the public for the opening of Giorgio Armani's first London store, ensuring that it became firmly fixed on the fashion shopper's map.

make-up artists and a fashion stylist commissioned and briefed.

Press releases

The press release is the most frequently used of all fashion PR tools. The release usually consists of an A4-size sheet containing brief details of a 'newsworthy' event such as the launch of a new line, a new collection or a new fragrance by a designer, along with the contact name and number of the PR director. These releases are circulated to all the editors who might have an interest in the story.

Once the information has been released by the PR office, it becomes harder to manage.

Magazine editors may alter the emphasis or omit certain information or even ignore it completely, since press releases must compete for editors' attention and editorial space with thousands of other press releases. Captioned photographs can help gain an editor's attention – if not editorial space. These photographs are organized by the PR office, and while the big 'glossies' can afford to commission their own choice of photographer to re-shoot the garments if they decide to follow up the PR's story, many 'lower-budget' fashion journals and much of the trade press, along with provincial newspapers, rely on PR photographs to illustrate their pages.

Photographs

Not all photographs generated by PRs are destined for feature articles: some are commissioned for window and showroom displays, for display in trade shows and travelling exhibitions and as 'set designs' for designer trunk shows and at press receptions. Other photographs may be destined for clients' corporate literature: company reports, annual accounts, staff training manuals and in-house journals –while others still are converted to 35mm slides for audio-visual presentations or for television stills during TV news bulletins.

Fashion shows

The event most closely associated with the fashion PR industry is the lavish, large-scale fashion show of the internationally famous designer. For the PR, handling this event is the ultimate accolade – and possibly the ultimate challenge. While it may be glamorous, the aim of the catwalk show in PR terms is to get coverage of the show in the world's press.

Depending on their client's wishes, the PR may also be involved in bringing together those who will contribute to the show: the producer, the stylist, the make-up and hair artists and the models.

The PR must decide which members of the press are invited and where each journalist, photographer and TV crew will be seated or placed and who will be allowed into the magic kingdom of 'backstage' after the show!

Because of the hierarchies in the press, PRs must be extremely knowledgeable of the pecking order! The editors of *American Vogue* and *Women's Wear Daily* and the fashion correspondent of the *International Herald Tribune* are accorded the best seats in the house. Getting John Fairchild himself (head of Fairchild Publications, the publishers of the fashion 'bible' *Women's Wear Daily*, *Fashion Guide*, *Women's Apparel Guide* and *Daily News Record*, among other titles) to attend a designer's show is the jewel in the PR's crown. An alternative strategy is to sprinkle the audience with a few celebrities who are suitably dressed in the designer's outfits.

Good seats at the shows are generally given to those journalists who received and reviewed the previous seasons' collections in a favourable manner! A bad review from a journalist can lead not just to a bad seat with a restricted view but to blacklisting and exclusion from the show altogether. This was what happened to former *London Evening Standard* fashion editor Lowri Turner when she once criticized a collection by the late Gianni Versace.

The PR begins work on the seating plan by calculating the number of available seats and using an updated and well-researched press list. Ticket request forms are sent to those journals and newspapers on the seating plan asking for a list of ticket requests in order of priority: if the magazine wants to send a large team to cover the show, there may not be enough room, and the more junior members of the team may be assigned standing-room-only places alongside journalists from the 'less important' journals.

Pre- and post-show interviews with the press have to be organized, and requests from the press

Catwalk presentation at Yves Saint Laurent. Organizing the lavish, large-scale fashion show of an internationally acclaimed designer is the ultimate challenge for the fashion PR.

have to be considered and weighed against the potential publicity aimed at the heart of the designer's target audience that such coverage will bring. Press packs have to be prepared: these include press releases, photographs and occasionally 'free gifts' of designer perfumes and accessories. While the show producer usually deals with the backstage activities, and the

wardrobe mistress and dressers and the designer's team handle the dress rails, steamers, irons and mirrors, the PR is usually responsible for 'feeding and watering' – the backstage catering and refreshments for the team and the press.

Once the show starts, the PR keeps one eye on the clothes and the other on the press to

One of the key activities of fashion PR is developing and maintaining good relations with the fashion press. Media heavyweights Grace Coddington (left) and Anna Wintour (right) are inevitably allocated seats with the best views at the collections.

gauge their reactions to each outfit. After the show the PR becomes a 'bouncer', making sure that the backstage area is secure from unofficial entry from the uninvited – usually fashion students masquerading as press, models and buyers! Although the show may be over, the fashion PR's job isn't. There are pictures to be chased up, sample garments to be sent to magazines for fashion shoots, articles and reviews to be gathered, clipped and filed for the designer's press book, and television footage to be videotaped into a compilation to be presented to their client and for possible use in retail stores. Finally, the PR has to provide merchandising information – prices, sizes, colours, styles and stockists for newspapers and magazines. PRs prioritize stockists, since stores that place the most orders get the most frequent credits.

In-store fashion shows, especially for bridal and evening wear, are often PR organized events which give customers information on designers, styles and trends.

Other events

While the catwalk shows remain fixed seasonal events of the fashion calendar, there are a number of other methods that fashion PRs can use to promote the designer's name or products. Guest appearances at stores by designers, in-store fashion shows – particularly for bridal and evening wear – prove successful vehicles for disseminating information about the designer,

the styles and the latest trends, and they are now common in major department stores.

Designer 'trunk shows' are also organized in conjunction with a single vendor and are a popular way to promote and sell more expensive lines. In the trunk show, the designer travels with the collection, which is shown on models in the store. Invited retail customers (often account customers or 'gold card' customers) can place orders for outfits which may not even be stocked by the store.

Other in-store events may take the form of exhibitions which are used to promote designs from a particular part of the world or in a

Timely PR activity arranged actress and model Liz Hurley in 'that dress' by Versace when publicity about her relationship with actor Hugh Grant was at its height.

particular fabric or fibre. Large-scale exhibitions are increasingly popular as a method of getting in contact directly with the target market. The largest exhibition in the UK is the BBC's Clothes Show Live event staged at the National Exhibition Centre in Birmingham, which includes catwalk fashion shows, make-over sessions, competitions and public participation, as well as being a forum for fashion design and showcasing fashion-related educational courses in the UK for young people who want to train for careers in the industry.

To demonstrate that the fashion industry is 'caring', PR offices are often involved in fundraising and consciousness-raising events. Charity balls offer the opportunity for designer outfits to be seen being worn by the rich and famous: the ensuing publicity from such events raises the designer's profile and helps to encourage contributions to charities like AIDS Research and Breast Cancer Awareness as well as demonstrating to the general public that despite appearances, the fashion industry is socially aware and responsible, even though it is concerned with the transient and often fickle nature of fashion.

PR IN THE FUTURE

If a fashion company is to market its products or services effectively, then fashion PR must play an important role in supporting the company's marketing strategies. If fashion PRs are to be as successful in the next millennium, they cannot afford to rest on their successes of the past. Like the fashion industry as a whole, they must be ready to respond to a whole host of new marketing problems, ranging from 'green issues' and the emerging economies of the Pacific Rim countries to the loss of the 'traditional' youth markets in the face of the 'Grey Revolution' (an ageing population with an increasing number of people being either redundant from work or taking early retirement).

By the year 2000, it is estimated that in the UK there will be close to 13 million people in the 50–69 age group, but only 10.5 million 15–29-year-olds. The impact of this change in consumer demographics on the fashion industry is likely to be profound, and we are already seeing PR companies respond to the change: alongside the babes and waifs on the catwalks are a number of 'more mature' models who ably demonstrate that being fashionable is not the preserve of the young.

READING LIST

Berkman, Harold W. and Christopher Gilson,
Consumer Behaviour: Concepts and Strategies, Kent Publishing, 1986

Celente, Gerald and Tom Milton,
Trend Tracking, John Wiley, 1990

Cobrin, A. Harry,
The Men's Clothing Industry – Colonial Through Modern Times, Fairchild Publications, 1970

Dichter, Ernst,
Handbook of Consumer Motivations, McGraw-Hill Book Co., 1964

Fairchild's Textile and Apparel Financial Directory, Fairchild Publications, Annual

Frings, Gini Stephens,
Fashion from Concept to Consumer, Prentice Hall, 1991

Gold, Annalee,
How to Sell Fashion, Fairchild Publications, Inc., 1968

Jarnow, Jeanette and Miriam Guerreiro,
Inside the Fashion Business, John Wiley, 1991

Kotler, Philip,
Principles of Marketing (3rd edition), Prentice Hall, 1986

Seidel, Leon E.,
Applied Textile Marketing, W.R.C Smith Publishing Co., 1971

Rogers, Dorothy, S. and Linda R. Gamans,
Fashion: A Marketing Approach, Holt, Rinehart and Winston, 1983

Wingate, Isabel B.,
Fairchild's Dictionary of Textiles, Fairchild Publications, 1979

Journal of Marketing
Journal of Marketing Research
Women's Wear Daily

PICTURE ACKNOWLEDGEMENTS

6 **Reproduced by permission of the Trustees of the Wallace Collection, London**; 8 **The National Gallery of Art, Washington DC, Timken Collection**, 10 **Adel Rootstein**; 11 **Private Collection**; 13 **Henry Poole and Co.**; 14 **Rex Features**; 16 **Rex Features**; 18 **Rex Features**; 19 **Rex Features**; 20 **Louis Vuitton**, 22 **Rex Features**; 25 **Rex Features**; 26 **Liz Claiborne**; 28 **Rex Features**; 31 **Rex Features**; 32 **Rex Features**; 35 **Rex Features**; 36 **Rex Features**; 37 **Rosemary Moore/Stowaway**; 39 **Lycra by Du Pont**; 40 **Lace with Lycra**; 42 **Home Laundering Consultative Council**; 43 **Rex Features**; 47 **Rex Features**; 48 [left] **Rex Features**; 48 [right] **Henry Poole and Co.**; 49 **Rex Features**; 50 **Rex Features**; 52 **Jantzen**; 53 **Liz Claiborne**; 54 **Dockers**; 55 **Lycra by Du Pont**; 58 **Rex Features**; 61 **Louis Vuitton**; 62 **Chanel**; 63 **Rex Features**; 64 **Aquascutum**; 67 [top] **Reebok**; 67 [left] **Lacoste**; 67 [right] **Louis Vuitton**; 69 **Rex Features**; 70 **Rex Features**; 73 **Rex Features**; 74 **Rex Features**; 76 **Rex Features**; 78 **Rex Features**; 80 **Rex Features**; 81 **Henry Poole and Co.**; 83 **Rex Features**; 88 **Rex Features**; 90 **Rex Features**; 91 **Rex Features**; 92 [left] **Rex Features**; 92 [right] **Rex Features**

Front cover: **Rex Features**

Back cover: **Louis Vuitton**

INDEX

age 22–4, 32, 93
alta moda 48–9
Armani, Giorgio 53, 70, 80
Aquascutum 63–4

Baker, Ted 6
Beene, Geoffrey 53
Benetton 57, 65–6
Bertin, Rose 9–10
Blass, Bill 53
Body Shop 19, 31, 57
Boss, Hugo 53, 66
brands 60–71
Burlington Industries 38
Butterick, Ebenezer 17
buying 76–81

Camera Nazionale dell'Alta Moda Italiana 48
Cardin, Pierre 15, 53, 57, 75
Cassini, Oleg 38
Chambre Syndicale de la Couture 12–14, 50
Chambre Syndicale de la Mode Masculine 13
Chambre Syndicale de la Pret-a-Porter 12, 15, 19, 46, 50
Chanel 16, 46, 62
chemical industries 18
Claibourne, Liz 27, 52–3
Color Association of America 44
colour trends 43–44
consumer behaviour 22–33
couture 15–19, 22, 46–9
couturier 9, 12–13

Demorest, Ellen & William 17
Designer Collective 55
Dior, Christian 16, 46, 48
distribution 56–9
Dockers 53–4
dolls 9
du Barry, Madame 9
Dunhill 62
DuPont 38, 40

Eastman Kodak 38, 40
EDI (Electronic Data Interchange) 45
electronic shopping 59
environment 42–3

Fairchild, John 76, 89
Fashion Monitor 86
Ferre, Gianfranco 48
Fila 20
forecasting 72–76
franchising 57
Franks, Lynne 82–3
French Connection 57
Fruit of the Loom 53

GATT 45
Gaultier, Jean Paul 9, 50
gender 24, 27
geodemographics 29
George IV 12
Givenchy 46
Gres, Alix 15

Hartnell, Norman 49
Hermes 63, 65
home sewing 17
Howe, Elias 17

ICI 38
Idea Como 44
IGEDO 51
IMBEX 51
income 27
International Color Authority 43–4
International Wool Secretariat 40–41
INTERSTOFF 44

Jantzen 45
JIT (Just In Time) 45
Josephine, Empress 11
Joseph Tricot 57

Karan, Donna 53, 70
Kelly, Patrick 50
Kenzo 50
Klein, Anne 38
Klein, Calvin 52–3, 70, 75

labelling 41–42
Lauder, Estee 62
Lauren, Ralph 53, 57, 75
Leroy, L.H 12
Levi-Strauss 20, 38, 53, 62–3
licensing 57–58
London Fashion Week 51
Louis XIV 6
Louis Vuitton 20, 63
Lycra 36, 38

mail order 58–9
mannequins 9–10
Marie Antoinette 8–9
marketing 20, 46–59
Marks & Spencer 38, 55, 62, 65
Maslow's hierarchy of needs 30–31
menswear 10–11, 12, 49–50
Men's Fashion Association 55
MFA (Multi Fibre Agreement) 45
Milanovendamoda Uomo 51
Miyake, Issey 22
moda pronta 48, 51
Mondi 57
MTV 17

Nike 20, 53, 66–7
Nouvelles Rencontres 44
Novotex 43
Nuno Corporation 43

Ortenberg, Arthur 52
occupation 25

paper patterns 17
Phillips Petroleum 38
Polyester Fashion Council 38
Pompadour, Madame de 6–7
Poole, Henry 12, 50, 80
Premier Vision 44
press events 87–8
Proctor & Gamble 68–9
public relations 82–93

Public Relation Society of America 84

QR (Quick Response) 45

Reebok 20, 53, 66–7
regenerated fibres 35
Renta, Oscar de la 53
Rogers, Jeffrey 55
Rolex 62
Rootstein, Adel 9

Saint Laurent, Yves 14, 46, 75, 90
Savile Row 12–13, 49–50
Scassi, Arnold 17
self-concept 32
silk 34
Singer, Isaac 17
Soviet jeans 86
Swatch 65–66
synthetic fibres 34–7

tailoring 16–17
Tie Rack 57
Tobe Associates 74

UPC (Universal Product Code) 45
Unilever 68

Valentino, Mario 48
Versace, Gianni 48, 76, 90, 92
VF Corporation 52, 62
video 75–76

wool 40–41
Woolmark 40–41
Woolworth, F.W 6
Worth, Charles Frederick 12
Wrangler jeans 52, 62

Yamamoto, Yohji 50